First World War
and Army of Occupation
War Diary
France, Belgium and Germany

63 (ROYAL NAVAL) DIVISION
Divisional Troops
Royal Army Medical Corps
148 Field Ambulance
1 June 1916 - 30 April 1919

WO95/3106/1

The Naval & Military Press Ltd
www.nmarchive.com
Published in association with The National Archives

Published by

The Naval & Military Press Ltd

Unit 10 Ridgewood Industrial Park,

Uckfield, East Sussex,

TN22 5QE England

Tel: +44 (0) 1825 749494

www.naval-military-press.com

www.nmarchive.com

This diary has been reprinted in facsimile from the original. Any imperfections are inevitably reproduced and the quality may fall short of modern type and cartographic standards.

© **Crown Copyright**
Images reproduced by permission of The National Archives, London, England, 2015.

Contents

Document type	Place/Title	Date From	Date To
Heading	WO95/3106/1		
Heading	63rd Division No.1. (R.N) Field Ambulance Jun 1916-jun 1917 (Became No. 148 (RN) Fld Amb. Jly 1917		
Heading	R.N.D. Division No. 1 (R.N.) Field Ambulance June1916		
Heading	War Diary of 1st Field Ambulance R.N Division From June 1st 1916 To June 30th 1916		
War Diary	Liercourt	01/06/1916	07/06/1916
War Diary	Hallencourt	08/06/1916	17/06/1916
War Diary	Bruay	17/06/1916	17/06/1916
War Diary	Monneville	18/06/1916	24/06/1916
War Diary	Ourton	25/06/1916	30/06/1916
Miscellaneous	A Form Messages And Signals		
Heading	War Diary of 1st Field Ambulance 63rd (R.N.) D From 1st July 1916 To 31st July 1916 Volume 2		
War Diary	Ourton	01/07/1916	17/07/1916
War Diary	Coupigny	17/07/1916	31/07/1916
Miscellaneous	A Form Messages And Signals		
Heading	War Diary of 1st Field Ambulance 63rd (R.N.) Divn From 1st August 1916 To 31st August 1916 Volume 3		
War Diary	Coupigny	01/08/1916	31/08/1916
Heading	War Diary of 1st Field Ambulance 63rd (R.N.) Divn From 1st September 1916 To 30th September 1916 Vol 4		
War Diary	Coupigny	01/09/1916	18/09/1916
War Diary	Fresnicourt	18/09/1916	30/09/1916
Miscellaneous	A Form Messages And Signals		
Heading	War Diary of 1st Field Ambulance Of 63rd (R.N.) Division From 1st October 1916 To 31st October 1916		
War Diary	Fresnicourt	01/10/1916	04/10/1916
War Diary	Forceville	05/10/1916	18/10/1916
War Diary	Varennes	18/10/1916	31/10/1916
Miscellaneous	Headquarters 63 (R.N.) Div 2 Oct 1916 Extract From 63 (RN) Div Medical Unit Operation Order No.8	08/10/1916	08/10/1916
Operation(al) Order(s)	Extract from 63 (RN) Division Medical Unit Operation Order No. 12	18/10/1916	18/10/1916
Miscellaneous	Medical Arrangements Combined Main Dressing Station of The Field Ambulance 63 (RN) Div The 48th Field Ambulance 37th Div	25/10/1916	25/10/1916
Miscellaneous	63rd (RN) Division Casualties Divisional Troops		
Miscellaneous	63rd (RN) Division Casualties, Infantry Brigade		
Heading	63rd Divn 1st R.N.D. Field Ambulance		
Heading	War Diary of 1st Field Ambulance 63 (R.N.) Divn From 1st November 1916 To 31st November 1916 Vol 6		
War Diary	Varennes	01/11/1918	17/11/1918
War Diary	Beauval	17/11/1918	18/11/1918
War Diary	Autheux	18/11/1918	20/11/1918
War Diary	Vacquerie	20/11/1918	21/11/1918
War Diary	Yvrench	21/11/1918	22/11/1918

War Diary	Fontaine-Sur-Maye	23/11/1918	23/11/1918
War Diary	Nouvion-En-Ponthieu	23/11/1918	24/11/1918
War Diary	Arry	24/11/1918	30/11/1918
Miscellaneous	A Form Messages And Signals		
Heading	War Diary of 1st Field Ambulance 63 (RN) Divn From 1st December 1916 To 31st December 1916 Vol 7		
War Diary	Arry	01/12/1916	12/12/1916
War Diary	Vron	12/12/1916	18/12/1916
War Diary	Nempont	18/12/1916	28/12/1916
War Diary	Nempont St. Firmin	28/12/1916	31/12/1916
Miscellaneous	A Form Messages And Signals		
Heading	War Diary of 1st Field Ambulance 63rd (R.N.) Division From 1st January To 31st January 1917 Vol 8		
War Diary	Nempont St. Firmin	01/01/1917	13/01/1917
War Diary	Nouvion	14/01/1917	14/01/1917
War Diary	Froyelles	15/01/1917	15/01/1917
War Diary	Le Meillard	16/01/1917	17/01/1917
War Diary	Beauquesnes	17/01/1917	18/01/1917
War Diary	Lancashire Dump	19/01/1917	21/01/1917
War Diary	Lame Dump	21/01/1917	28/01/1917
War Diary	Lancashire Dump	29/01/1917	31/01/1917
Heading	War Diary of 1st Field Ambulance 63rd (R.N.) Divn From 1st February 1917 To 28th February 1917 Vol 9		
War Diary	Lancashire Dump	01/02/1917	17/02/1917
War Diary	Lame Dump	18/02/1917	18/02/1917
War Diary	Lancashire Dump	19/02/1917	28/02/1917
Heading	War Diary of 1st Field Ambulance 63rd (R.N.) Division From 1st March 1917 To 31st March 1917 Vol10		
War Diary	Lancashire Dump	01/03/1917	17/03/1917
War Diary	Warloy	18/03/1917	18/03/1917
War Diary	Herissart	19/03/1917	19/03/1917
War Diary	Bretel	20/03/1917	20/03/1917
War Diary	Fortel	21/03/1917	21/03/1917
War Diary	Gauchin	22/03/1917	23/03/1917
War Diary	Cauchy A La-Tour	24/03/1917	24/03/1917
War Diary	St. Hilaire	25/03/1917	25/03/1917
War Diary	Calonne Sur-La-Lys	26/03/1917	28/03/1917
War Diary	Labourse	29/03/1917	31/03/1917
Heading	No.1. R.N. F.A.		
Heading	B.E.F. Summary of Medical War Diaries For 1st R.N. 63rd R.N. Divn.13th Corps 1st Army 3rd Army From 11/4/17 Western Front April-may '17.		
Miscellaneous	Phase "B" Battle Of Arras-April-May 1917 1st Period Attack On Vimy Ridge April.	30/04/1917	30/04/1917
War Diary	La Bourse	01/04/1917	11/04/1917
War Diary	Ourton	11/04/1917	14/04/1917
War Diary	X Hutments Ecoivres	14/04/1917	22/04/1917
War Diary	St. Catherines	22/04/1917	30/04/1917
Heading	Cover For Documents. Nature Of Enclosures Pathology 9. Pneumonia		
Heading	War Diary 1st Field Ambulance 63rd (R.N.) Division From 1st May 1917 To 31st May 1917 Vol 12		
Heading	Summary Of Medical War Diaries For 1st R.N /63rd R.N. Divn. 13th Corps 1st Army 3rd Army From 11/4/17 Western Front April-May. 17		

Miscellaneous	Phase "B" Battle Of Arras-April-May 1917 2nd Period Capture Of Siegfried Line May		
Miscellaneous	Phase "B" Battle Of Arras-April-May 1917 2nd Period Capture Of Siegfried Line May	01/05/1917	01/05/1917
War Diary	Maroeuil	01/05/1917	01/05/1917
War Diary	Frevillers	02/05/1917	08/05/1917
War Diary	Cambligneul	09/05/1917	20/05/1917
War Diary	St, Catherines	21/05/1917	31/05/1917
Heading	War Diary of 1st (R.N.) Field Ambulance 63rd (RN) Division From 1st June 1917 To 30th June 1917		
War Diary	St. Catherines	01/06/1917	11/06/1917
War Diary	Cambligneul	12/06/1917	30/06/1917
Heading	63rd Division No.148th (R.N.) Fld Ambulance 1916 Jun-1919 Apl		
Heading	War Diary of No 148. (Royal Naval) Field Ambulance 63rd. (R.N.) D. From 1st July To 31st July 1917 Vol 14		
War Diary	Cambligneul	01/07/1917	02/07/1917
War Diary	Anzin	03/07/1917	31/07/1917
Heading	War Diary of the 148th (Royal Naval) Field Ambulance For The Period 1st To 31st August 1917 Vol 15		
War Diary	Anzin	01/08/1917	31/08/1917
Heading	War Diary of 148th (Royal Naval) Field Ambulance For The Period. 1st September 1917 To 30th September 1917; Inclusive Vol 16		
War Diary	Anzin	01/09/1917	05/09/1917
War Diary	Maroeuil	06/17/1917	22/09/1917
War Diary	Averdoing	23/09/1917	23/09/1917
War Diary	Houvelin	24/09/1917	30/09/1917
Heading	War Diary of 148th (R.N.) Field Ambulance For Period 1st. October 1917 To 31st. October 1917		
War Diary	Houvelin	01/10/1917	03/10/1917
War Diary	7 Camp A16.c.5.3 Sheet 2.8	04/10/1917	16/10/1917
War Diary	A.23.C.2.9 Map Ref. Sheet 28.	17/10/1917	23/10/1917
War Diary	C.17d.2.6 Map Ref. Sheet 28	24/10/1917	28/10/1917
War Diary	A.23.C.2.9 Sheet 28.	29/10/1917	31/10/1917
Heading	War Diary of the 148th (Royal Naval) Field Ambulance Covering The Period 1st November, 1917 To 30th November, 1917		
War Diary	C17d.2.6 Sheet 28	01/11/1917	07/11/1917
War Diary	A 23.c.9 Sheet 28	08/11/1917	08/11/1917
War Diary	School Camp L.3 (Sheet 27)	09/11/1917	11/11/1917
War Diary	Winnezeele J 16.0 Sheet 27	12/11/1917	13/11/1917
War Diary	Ledringhem C26b8.1 Sheet 27	13/11/1917	19/11/1917
War Diary	Ledringhem C 27a7.6	20/11/1917	28/11/1917
War Diary	D24b9.7 Sheet 27	28/11/1917	30/11/1917
Heading	War Diary of the 148th (Royal Naval) Field Ambulance For The Period 1st December 1917 To 31st December, 1917 Vol 19		
War Diary	D24.b.9.7 Sheet 27	01/12/1917	05/12/1917
War Diary	7.27.c Sheet 27	06/12/1917	09/12/1917
War Diary	Le. Transloy Camp	10/12/1917	13/12/1917
War Diary	Rocquigny	14/12/1917	14/12/1917
War Diary	Manancourt	15/12/1917	15/12/1917
War Diary	Barastre	16/12/1917	31/12/1917

Heading	War Diary of the 148th (Royal Naval) Field Ambulance For The Period 1st January 1918 To 31st January 1918 Vol 20		
War Diary	Barastre	01/01/1918	31/01/1918
Heading	No. 148. F.A.		
Heading	War Diary of 148th (Royal Naval) Field Ambulance From 1st February 1918 To 28th February 1918 Vol 21		
War Diary	Barastre	01/02/1918	13/02/1918
War Diary	Metz (Q20. C 6.9 Sheet 57c	14/02/1918	18/02/1918
War Diary	Metz (Q20.C6.9)	19/02/1918	28/02/1918
War Diary	Metz (Q20 C 6.9) Sheet 57 C	28/02/1918	28/02/1918
Heading	148. F.A. March 1918		
War Diary	Metz Q20. C.6.9	01/03/1918	10/03/1918
War Diary	Q14C.8.8	11/03/1918	21/03/1918
War Diary	Ruyaulcourt P.10 Central Sheet 57.C	22/03/1918	23/03/1918
War Diary	Le. Transloy CN24d 5.5 Fricourt	24/03/1918	24/03/1918
War Diary	Bouzincourt (W.Y.c.6.5 57.D)	25/03/1918	25/03/1918
War Diary	Bouzincourt	25/03/1918	25/03/1918
War Diary	Le Alvillers (O.23.b.5.7.57.D)	26/03/1918	31/03/1918
Heading	148th Field Ambulance April 1918		
Heading	War Diary of the 148th (Royal Naval) Field Ambulance For The Period 1st April 1918 To 30th April, 1918		
War Diary	Lealvillers O23b.5.7 Sheet 57d	01/04/1918	03/04/1918
War Diary	Clairfaye (O.29.b.6.9 Sheet 57D)	04/04/1918	14/04/1918
War Diary	Puchevillers (N28a.9.4 Sheet 57D)	15/04/1918	30/04/1918
Heading	War Diary of the 148th (Royal Naval) Field Ambulance For The Period, 1st May, 1918 To 31st May, 1918 Vol 24		
War Diary	Puchevillers N 28.A.9.4 Sheet 57D	01/05/1918	08/05/1918
War Diary	Clairfaye O.29.b 6.9	09/05/1918	31/05/1918
Heading	War Diary of the 148th (Royal Naval) Field Ambulance For The Period 1st. June, 1918 To 30th June, 1918		
War Diary	Clairfaye O.29.b.6.9	01/06/1918	05/06/1918
War Diary	Herissart T.10.a.4.4	06/06/1918	08/06/1918
War Diary	Herissart	09/06/1918	22/06/1918
War Diary	Acheux P.13.d.4.3	23/06/1918	30/06/1918
Heading	War Diary of the 148th (Royal Naval) Field Ambulance For The Period 1st July 1918 To 31st July 1918		
War Diary	Acheux P.13.d.4.3	01/07/1918	25/07/1918
War Diary	Le. Menage	26/07/1918	29/07/1918
War Diary	Mont Renault Farm Lens II 5.C.	30/07/1918	31/07/1918
Heading	War Diary of the 148th (Royal Naval) Field Ambulance For The Period 1st, August, 1918 To 31st. August, 1918		
War Diary	Mt Renault Farm (Lens II 5 C)	01/08/1918	06/08/1918
War Diary	Le Menage	07/08/1918	09/08/1918
War Diary	Contay U.26 b 2.8 Sheet 57 D	10/08/1918	14/08/1918
War Diary	Henu Wood O16 D Sheet 57D	15/08/1918	16/08/1918
War Diary	Citadelle Doullens	17/08/1918	19/08/1918
War Diary	Henu Wood C 24b 3.5	20/08/1918	20/08/1918
War Diary	D 26 B Sheet 57 D	21/08/1918	22/08/1918
War Diary	Citadelle Doullens	23/08/1918	31/08/1918
Heading	War Diary of 148th (Royal Naval) Field Ambulance, From:- 1st September 1918 To:- 30th September 1918.		
War Diary	Boiry. St. Rictrude Map Ref S.9.C. Sheet 51B SW	01/09/1918	01/09/1918
War Diary	Cagnicourt V13.C.3.5 Sheet 51 B	02/09/1918	03/09/1918

War Diary	V.15.C.8.4 Sheet 51 B	04/09/1918	07/09/1918
War Diary	Gouy-En-Artois	08/09/1918	16/09/1918
War Diary	Blairville X4a.7.3 Sheet 51 C	17/09/1918	17/09/1918
War Diary	U25a. Sheet 57 B	18/09/1918	18/09/1918
War Diary	V.25.a Sheet 57 B	19/09/1918	25/09/1918
War Diary	J.4 C Sheet 57 C	26/09/1918	27/09/1918
War Diary	E29.a.6.8 Sheet 57c (Sugar Factory)	28/09/1918	28/09/1918
War Diary	Anneux 7.25.a.3.7 Sheet 57 C	29/09/1918	30/09/1918
Heading	War Diary of the 148th (Royal Naval) Field Ambulance For The Period 1st October, 1918 To 31st October, 1918 Vol 29		
War Diary	Anneux 7 25a.3.7 Sheet 57 C	01/10/1918	06/10/1918
War Diary	Noyelles	07/10/1918	07/10/1918
War Diary	Chateau L 11 B 5.5 Sheet 57 C	07/10/1918	07/10/1918
War Diary	Noyelles	08/10/1918	08/10/1918
War Diary	Anneux	09/10/1918	09/10/1918
War Diary	Morchies I 6 B Sheet 57 C	10/10/1918	11/10/1918
War Diary	Siracourt	12/10/1918	21/10/1918
War Diary	Gouy-En-Ternois	22/10/1918	31/10/1918
Heading	War Diary of the 148th (R.N.) Field Ambulance For The Period 1st November 1918 To 30th November 1918		
War Diary	Evin Malmaison	01/11/1918	04/11/1918
War Diary	Haulchin	05/11/1918	05/11/1918
War Diary	Aulnoy	06/11/1918	06/11/1918
War Diary	Saultain	07/11/1918	07/11/1918
War Diary	Angre	08/11/1918	08/11/1918
War Diary	Audregnies	09/11/1918	12/11/1918
War Diary	Nouvelles	13/11/1918	17/11/1918
War Diary	Valenciennes	18/11/1918	30/11/1918
Heading	War Diary Medical 148th (R.N.) Field Ambulance From 1st December 1918 To 31st December 1918		
War Diary	Valencienne	01/12/1918	13/12/1918
War Diary	Paturages	14/12/1918	31/12/1918
Heading	63rd Div Box 2985 War Diary 148th (Royal Naval) Field Ambulance From 1st January 1919 To 31st January 1919		
War Diary	Paturages	01/01/1919	31/01/1919
Heading	War Diary of 148 (RN) Field Ambulance From : 1st February 1919 To 28th February 1919		
War Diary	Paturages	01/02/1919	28/02/1919
Heading	War Diary of 148 (RN) Field Ambulance From 1st March 1919 To 31st March 1919		
War Diary	Paturages	01/03/1919	31/03/1919
Heading	War Diary of 148 (Royal Naval) Field Ambulance From 1st April 1919 To 30th April 1919		
War Diary	Paturages	01/04/1919	30/04/1919

100 95/3106/1

63RD DIVISION

NO.1. (R.N) FIELD AMBULANCE
JUN 1916 - JUN 1917
(BECAME NO.148(RN) FLD AMB. JLY 1917

R.N.D. Division

No. 1 (R.N.) Field Ambulance.

June 1916.

June 5 NO 1 & arot VOL 1

1st FIELD AMBULANCE, ROYAL NAVAL DIV.
No.
Date 30th June 1916.

"CONFIDENTIAL"

WAR DIARY

of

1ST FIELD AMBULANCE R.N. DIVISION.

From

June 1st 1916

To.

June 30th 1916.

To. A.G's Office
 3rd Echelon.

A. F. Fleming.
Staff Surgeon R.N.
O.C. 1st Field Amb^ce
R.N. Division

WAR DIARY
or
INTELLIGENCE SUMMARY.
(Erase heading not required.)

Army Form C. 2118.

Place	Date	Hour	Summary of Events and Information	Remarks and references to Appendices
LIERCOURT	1.6.16		1st Field Ambulance. R.N. Division arrived at PONT REMY Station on 23rd May from IMBROS via MARSEILLES and went into billets at LIERCOURT. Proceeded to make up for mobilization stores to complete. Personnel - 8 officers, 182 O.R.	Off.
LIERCOURT	2.6.16		40 gas helmets for drill purposes received. Officers of Sub divisions take N.C.O.s and men in instruction of them. Lectures given them all ranks in turn had Gas Helmet drill. 2. Gas Helmets & one pair goggles issued to each Officer and O.R.s Letter from Routine order 31/5/16 No 0078. One man or Officer allowed 8 days leave to England from Field ambulance. Only urgent cases allowed to go.	Off.
LIERCOURT	3.6.16		Route marching and General Routine carried out.	Off.
LIERCOURT	4.6.16		The following Transport & personnel arrived from ABBEVILLE were taken on charge 1st Field ambulance.	Off.
LIERCOURT	5.6.16			

	Draught	Heavy draught	Riding
Horses	21	18	13

Personnel	Sergts	Cpls	Ptes
	2	1	32

WAR DIARY or INTELLIGENCE SUMMARY

Army Form C. 2118.

Place	Date	Hour	Summary of Events and Information	Remarks and references to Appendices
LIERCOURT	JUNE 6th		Writing approval received and stores ready	O.T.T.
"	7		Route marches. Lectures and instruction	
"			Orders received from Brigadier. Several moved to 1st R.N. Brigade T.M.B. 1st line	
HALLENCOURT	8		An Ernoux met bath at HALLENCOURT on 8th June	O.T.T. See appx /
"	9		arrived HALLENCOURT at 2.20 p.m. men billeted. Routine same as at LIERCOURT No 1	
"	10		Staff Sergeant Carr White pursuant in exchange approved 15 January 1915. Sen's [?] A.T.S. for instruction	O.T.T.
"	11		Bar Nos bags left for ABBEVILLE in S.R. waggons. Instruction in Intents. Revenue for Route march. Instructions and Sec Lieut Anell O.T.T.	
"	12		Routine. N.S. Browns Awloh Jos. Hulkwell Smith C.R.E. Tent instruction. Lecture on Pneumo O.T.T.	
		8/1800	Pte J. Howell removed Train attached 1st Field Amb. Craig - Struthers struck off strength - Six days Not field Punishment	
"	13	5/3862	Pte Hyles 1st Field Ambl. returned awaiting from leave England. A Tent Lecture & instruction	O.T.T.
"	14		Routine Rt Tents for Route march. A Tent Lecture & instruction	O.T.T.
			Move - Ambulance to be proposed to move all about notice. Stores to be enabled and ready for stowing in waggons	O.T.T.

T.131. Wt. W708-776. 500000. 4/16. Sir J.C. & S.

WAR DIARY or INTELLIGENCE SUMMARY

Army Form C. 2118.

(Erase heading not required.)

Instructions regarding War Diaries and Intelligence Summaries are contained in F.S. Regs., Part II. and the Staff Manual respectively. Title pages will be prepared in manuscript.

Place	Date	Hour	Summary of Events and Information	Remarks and references to Appendices
HALLENCOURT	June 15th		Orders received from O.C. 1st R.N. Brigade That Ambulance will entrain on Saturday 17th June at TRIAGE, ABBEVILLE	off
"	16		Routine – Packing Wagons ready, Entraine	off
"	17		Left HALLENCOURT 9 am. arrived ABBEVILLE 12.45 pm. Entrained left ABBEVILLE 6.25 pm	See Copy No 2 off
BRUAY	18		Arrived BRUAY 11 pm detrained. Proceeded with 4 cars to bullets at MONNEVILLE	
MONNEVILLE	18		Arrived MONNEVILLE 3 am. Balance men transport cleared up billets	
"	19		Inspected necessary stores. Surgeon Carr returned from instruction on Army auto San School. Attd Surgeon Quartus Stratton temporarily attached. Sheuld Wretin [?] Revds Behind 3rd R.N. Brigade by orders from Osmond R.N.D. Routine. Route march for all Sub Divisions Beanu Sub Division auto car Helmut Gres	off
"	20		A Section Bay Stafflergal Cars on auto sea drive ambulance to A Section Attd	off
"	21		B Section return by Stafflergal Cars Tents pitched for receiving patients from Attd 1st R.N. Brigade	
"	22		C Section return by Staufflergal Cars. A&B Tent Subs march	off
"	23		B Section with Surgeons Heather Hay Maunders Odum with park & no other Stores left at 9 am	

T/134. Wt. W708-776. 500000. 4/15. Sir J. C. & S.

WAR DIARY or INTELLIGENCE SUMMARY

Army Form C. 2118.

Place	Date	Hour	Summary of Events and Information	Remarks and references to Appendices
MONNEVILLE	June 22nd		From 2, 11, A.B.C. 13 report all 6 London Field Ambulances for further orders (Ref. instr. 36th & 4th B.) instructions received in extra which the ambulances number in 4.9 wagon accompanying Section containing panties & Officers baggage orders for move received from Colonel R.M.S. also orders received from A-Soins R.N.S. & that the remainder H.C. Ambulance was move into Bulli on DURTON on Saturday 24th; and 3 No. tents for Treating our Seaker Cases from R.N. Div. also to establish a hospital in a barn close by to treat cases from R.N. Division	See Copy No. 3/4
"	23rd		Received Routine orders No.1436 & fries in Bulli; required in Troops Saved A.T.T. and to all ranks. Preparing 3 lorries re for move	A.T.T.
"	24th		Ambulances with Transport left MONNEVILLE at 1-30 p.m. for DURTON arriving at DURTON at 3-45 p.m. Tents pitched; Barn prepared for reception of patients	A.T.T.
DURTON	25th		Cleaning up Bulli & preparing barn for Sick received	A.T.T.
"	26th		Tents ready for reception of Seaken patients; Bearers in building the used for patients & personnel of Field ambulances. Capt Thompson Nations from lunch	A.T.T.

Army Form C. 2118.

WAR DIARY
or
INTELLIGENCE SUMMARY.
(Erase heading not required.)

Instructions regarding War Diaries and Intelligence Summaries are contained in F. S. Regs., Part II. and the Staff Manual respectively. Title pages will be prepared in manuscript.

Place	Date	Hour	Summary of Events and Information	Remarks and references to Appendices
BURTON	June 27th		Routine - Auto Sea Helmets issued for all ranks now employed on duty.	off
"	28		Routine - Inspection of personnel for Scabies all hands who have not used Bath to take in use for detailing parade at 1-30 pm	off
"	29		Routine - Stand by for inspection by 10 corps Commander at 12 noon. Auto Sea Helmets issued	off
"	30		Routine - A Team to take in scraps drain for 4 days. Auto Sea helmet issued for attached Transport ratings at 1-30 pm	off

A.F. Hurst
Staff Surgeon Rn
OC 1st Field Ambulance
R.N. Division

"A" Form. Army Form C. 2121.
MESSAGES AND SIGNALS.

Prefix..........Code..........m. | Words | Charge | This message is on a/c of: | Recd. at............m.
Office of Origin and Service Instructions. | Sent At............m. | | ....Service. | Date....................
Copy | To............ | | | From....................
No. 1 | By............ | | (Signature of "Franking Officer.") | By....................

TO { C.C. 1st Field Ambulance
       R.N. Division.

Sender's Number: Q69/16　Day of Month: 6.6.16　In reply to Number:　AAA

The G.O.C. area wishes the 1st and 3rd Field Ambulances to move into billets in HALLENCOURT on Thursday 8th inst aaa The Brigade Interpreter will visit you tomorrow morning at 11 o'clock to make the necessary arrangements for billeting AAA

From: Staff Captain
Place: 1st R.N. Brigade
Time:

"A" Form.
Army Form C. 2121.

MESSAGES AND SIGNALS.

No. of Message_____

Prefix......Code......m.	Words	Charge	This message is on a/c of:	Recd. at........m.
Office of Origin and Service Instructions.				Date............
Copy	Sent		............Service.	From............
No 11	At......m.			
	To			By............
	By	(Signature of "Franking Officer.")		

TO { O.C. 1st Field Ambulance R.N.D.

| Sender's Number | Day of Month | In reply to Number | |
| Q 141/16 | 13.6.16 | | A A A |

The following billeting parties are to be detailed by Units. They will proceed to 1st Army Area on 15th inst. reporting to Personnel TRACE, ABBEVILLE at 9 pm 14th inst. Rations for 15th & 16th will be taken on arrival at BRUAY the parties will report to Town Major, Bruay.

1st Field Ambulance 1 Officer 1 NCO

From Staff Captain
Place 1st R N Brigade
Time

The above may be forwarded as now corrected. (Z)

"A" Form. Army Form C. 2121.
MESSAGES AND SIGNALS.

Copy
No 3

TO 1st Field Ambulance R.N.D

Sender's Number: F 389
Day of Month: 22/6/16
AAA

Send an advance Billeting party and tent pitching party to T34.a.4.9 tomorrow aaa Unoccupied tents should be struck and brought along for pitching aaa Remainder of Field Ambulance will move to above place on following day aaa

From A.D.M.S
Place R.N.D.

F. Casement Capt.

"A" Form. Army Form C. 2121.
MESSAGES AND SIGNALS.

No 4

TO: O/C 1st F A

Sender's Number: F.383.
Day of Month: 22/6/16.

AAA

You are to send tomorrow afternoon a section with 3 Officers to undergo training with the 47th Division aaa. Place to report at will be communicated later aaa.

From ADMS
Time 11 am

MEDICAL

"CONFIDENTIAL"

63 July - 1 amb - Vol 2

1st FIELD AMBULANCE, ROYAL NAVAL DIV:
No.
Date 1/8/16

WAR DIARY.

OF

1ST FIELD AMBULANCE 63RD (R.N) D.

FROM

1st JULY 1916

To

31st JULY 1916

Volume 2.

STAFF SURGEON, R.N.
O.C. 1ST FIELD AMBCE. R.N.D.

To/
D.N.Q.
63rd (R.N) Division

COMMITTEE FOR THE
MEDICAL HISTORY OF THE WAR
Date 5 - SEP 1916

WAR DIARY or INTELLIGENCE SUMMARY

Army Form C. 2118.

Place	Date	Hour	Summary of Events and Information	Remarks and references to Appendices
OURTON	July 1st		B Section arrived from COUPIGNY after undergoing weeks training in Section occupied by 6th & 4th London Field Ambulances. C. Section on route march. 9 C. A. Bulley 3/3215 joined ambulance from Sanitary Section & posted to C. Bearer Sub-division.	
OURTON	2nd		C. Section under Surgeon Case Eyes or & arm for COUPIGNY for 7 days training. Orders issued that all cases if admitted to testified ambulance are at least their other clothes examined for lice & also body inspection for scabies.	Signal No. 1
do.	3rd		The N.C.O's of B Section to stand in a short report is the orderly room by 9 am on 5th inst of their experiences when training under 6 & 4 London Field Ambulance & any suggestions or improvement brought forward. Sec N Cox to report on their different duties.	
do.	4th		All ranks not employed on duty or fatigues instructed under Sergt Elliott in Gas Helmet Drill.	
do.	5th		Sergt Nicholson & 6 men from B Bearers take over duties in Section Hospital Section B. for Routine work under Surgn Kay-Mouat. B Tent Subdivision duty in hospital.	

T.134. Wt. W708-776. 50,000. 4/15. Sir J.C. & S.

Army Form C. 2118.

WAR DIARY
or
INTELLIGENCE SUMMARY.
(Erase heading not required.)

Instructions regarding War Diaries and Intelligence Summaries are contained in F.S. Regs., Part II. and the Staff Manual respectively. Title pages will be prepared in manuscript.

Place	Date	Hour	Summary of Events and Information	Remarks and references to Appendices
DURTON.	July 6"		Surgeon E.G. Schlesinger returned to duty from leave in England. LIEUT. HAMELIN R.A.M.C. and CAPTAIN CRAIG, R.A.M.C. posted to 1st Field Ambulance (63rd (R.N) Division on 4th July. Capt Craig posted to B. (a) W Subdivision. Lieut. Hamelin to C. (c) Subdivision.	
Do.	7"		A. Section Route March under Surgeon Kay Brown. Field Medical Cards (Army Form w. 3118). to be properly filled in & to accompany all patients to F.A.B. & D.R.S.	
Do.	8"		2. G.S. Wagon to leave at 3 p.m. 15 living truck baggage. 2nd C. Section from COUPIGNY on Sunday 9" inst. Route March for all ranks not employed on fatigues and duty, under Capt Kay.	
Do.	9"		C. Section under Surgeon Coxe arrived here from COUPIGNY after undergoing 7 days training in trenches. A Section under Surgeons Ritchie and Hamelin left at 6 am for COUPIGNY for 7 days training in trenches attached to 188th Infantry Field Ambulance. e Tent Sub division take on duties at Hospitals 9 a.m.	
Do.	10"		one N.C.O. & 6 men from E. Beaver duty, or sent to hospitals.	

WAR DIARY
or
INTELLIGENCE SUMMARY.

(Erase heading not required.)

Army Form C. 2118.

Place	Date	Hour	Summary of Events and Information	Remarks and references to Appendices
OURTON	JULY 11th		Routine — Fatigues Antigas helmets issued	
Do.	12th		Routine. Fatigues	
Do.	13th		Routine. Fatigues. Reinforcements for all not employed on duty	
Do.	14th		Routine " " " " "	
Do.	15th		Routine " " " " "	
			B Tent. hut chimneys built, at Hospital. Preparation made for move. Orders dated 17th inst. directing to be made into 15.17th	
			A. Section to remain at COUPIGNY.	
			A Section Tents over A.D.S. and Bearer posts from 6 "London Field Ambulance".	
Do.	16		B Section with mobilisation stores moved at 4.35 pm from OURTON and took over Main Dressing Station of 6th London Field Amb at COUPIGNY at 9 pm. Surgeon Walker and Surgeon Mayhew Adam left with Section for duty with Section. Surgeon Wickes on arrival at COUPIGNY to proceed to A.D.S at AIX-NOULETTE. and assume charge of R Section. Corpl Crury to proceed from AIX-NOULETTE to main dressing station at COUPIGNY for duty with B Section	See copy of Signal No. 2

WAR DIARY
or
INTELLIGENCE SUMMARY

Army Form C. 2118.

Place	Date	Hour	Summary of Events and Information	Remarks and references to Appendices
OURTON	July 16th		Preparing stores for move to COURIGNY tomorrow. Patients now in hospital to be conveyed in Ambulances to COURIGNY tomorrow on 8.15 a.m. Ambulance wch starts transport is leave cmg. 30 am on 17th for main dressing station at Château COURIGNY.	
OURTON	17th		Left for COURIGNY at 8.30 am. Advance party from 100 Field Ambulance 2nd Divn took over hospital at OURTON.	See copy of Signal No 2
COURIGNY	18th		Arrived at COURIGNY at 12.45 p.m. 6 London Field Ambulance Hospital closed. Bre N.C.O. and of Chateau. B Tent Subdivision to move in Tents pitched in grounds of Château for Witnesses of Speakers	
			Fatigues clearing up grounds of hospital.	
B O.	19th		Surgeon Kay Hunter proceeds to A.D.S. aine NOUETTE from ADS to main dressing station COURIGNY	
B O.	20th		Weaving fatigues. Fumigation to be started for clothing of febrile patients	
B O.	21st		Weaving fatigues. Two Tent Subdivision to be on duty at main dressing station	

WAR DIARY
or
INTELLIGENCE SUMMARY.
(Erase heading not required.)

Army Form C. 2118.

Instructions regarding War Diaries and Intelligence Summaries are contained in F. S. Regs., Part II. and the Staff Manual respectively. Title pages will be prepared in manuscript.

Place	Date	Hour	Summary of Events and Information	Remarks and references to Appendices
COUPIGNY	JULY 22nd		Designation — The Royal Naval Division will in future be known as the 63rd (RN) Division. 1st Naval Brigade becomes 188th Brigade. 2nd " " " 189th " 3rd " " " 190th "	
			Medical order. MOs of Battalions are asked in a weekly report by 9 am each Saturday which are/results. Same sick return completed. All Officers to instead order Book + after name of men/name in Contents of form.	
			Three Officers to sleep in Château + be called if necessary by hospital ward master. and Banin Post.	
COUPIGNY	23rd		Necessary Polignin. B Section will relieve A Section at ADS leaving main Dressing station at 8 am on 24th for ADS.	
Do.	24th		B Section left for ADS Travern forde at 6 am. Section arrived at Main Dressing station COUPIGNY at 3 pm on being relieved by B Section.	
Do.	25th		Necessary Polignin. Canteen started for the personnel + patients (walking MO). Two officers + 28 NCOs men from B Section ambulance (63 The Bus) sent off for instruction + were sent up to ADS + Banin Post.	See copy of signed file 3

T.131. Wt. W708-776. 500,000. 4/15. Sir J. C. & S.

WAR DIARY
or
INTELLIGENCE SUMMARY

Army Form C. 2118.

(Erase heading not required.)

Place	Date	Hour	Summary of Events and Information	Remarks and references to Appendices
COURIGNY	July 26th		Necessary fatigues. Improving Sanitation of buildings. Wash places and latrines	
Do.	27th		Draining overhead Latrines. Burning refuse. Improving wash places	
"	28th		Inspection of Tentages by O.C. 63rd (Can.) Divisional Train. Watched them entrain Chateau prisoners by day. Necessary fatigues. Covered in bath house for patients personnel.	
"	29th		Necessary fatigues. Reconnaissances made out.	
"	30th		Pte. T.H. Wilson 3/1571 Divisional Train attached 1st Field Ambulance B3 "A.m} Divn" promoted Provisional Lance Corpl. (unpaid) 15th Oct. 30th July	
"	31st		C. Section med Relieve B Section at Brown Road & Potts Communication. 1st August leaving main dressing station at 8 a.m. for R.A.P.s. Men marched up with bands. Officers engage to protect new section. Surgeon Coe & Lieut Hamilton to write Section.	

B.F. Fleming
Major Surgeon i/c
O.C. 1st Field Ambul.

"A" Form.
Army Form C. 2121.
MESSAGES AND SIGNALS.

TO: O.C. 1st F a R N D

Sender's Number: F567
Day of Month: 1-7-16

AAA

Please detail a section for training with 47th Division to report to O/C 6th London Amb'ce on Sunday AAA It is arranged that your other section should return today AAA You will send Suffern to be in charge of the section proceeding AAA

From: Medical
Place: Naval
Time: 11.0 AM

Sdr E Finch Fleet Surg'n RN

"A" Form.
MESSAGES AND SIGNALS.

Army Form C. 2121.

TO: Staff Surgn Hemmy RN.

Day of Month: 15-7-16

Be prepared to take over 6th London FA Advanced Dressing Station and Bearer Posts with one section this afternoon AAA You are to visit O.C. 6th FA personally and make arrangements AAA Men can be got under way immediately taking full equipment with them. The whole of the 6th London FA. to be taken over by Monday next AAA

From: Medical (D.A.D.M.S.)
Place: Naval
Time: 1-0 p.m.

"A" Form.
MESSAGES AND SIGNALS.
Army Form C. 2121.

TO: O.C. 1st Fd Amb

Sender's Number: F924   AAA

Propose to attach two officers with half a brace and half a tent sub-division to your Advanced Dressing Station from the 2nd F.A. in order that they may acquire a knowledge of the work of the Advanced Dressing Station & the locality AAA They will join yours on Tuesday morning and bring rations for Tuesday & Wednesday AAA Please arrange accommodation AAA

From: ADMS
Place:
Time: 2.30 pm

MEDICAL.

1st FIELD AMBULANCE, ROYAL NAVAL DIV.
No.........
Date 1 Sept. 1916.

COMMITTEE FOR THE MEDICAL HISTORY OF THE WAR
Date -9 OCT. 1916

"CONFIDENTIAL."
VOLUME 3.

WAR DIARY

of

1ST FIELD AMBULANCE 63RD (R.N) DIVN

from

1ST AUGUST 1916

to

31ST AUGUST 1916.

A. F. Fleming
STAFF SURGEON, R.N.
O.O. 1ST FIELD AMBCE, R.N.D.
63RD (R.N) Divn.

Army Form C. 2118.

FIELD AMBULANCE, ROYAL NAVAL DIV. 1st

WAR DIARY
or
INTELLIGENCE SUMMARY.
(Erase heading not required.)

Instructions regarding War Diaries and Intelligence Summaries are contained in F. S. Regs., Part II. and the Staff Manual respectively. Title pages will be prepared in manuscript.

Place	Date	Hour	Summary of Events and Information	Remarks and references to Appendices
COUVIGNY	1916. August 1st		Surgeon Lieut Hamelin with C Section left at 8 am. Chain Dressing Station. J to relieve B Section at the Advanced Dressing Station & Bearer Relay Post.	
AD.S.	2nd		Relief by Medical Officers Sub-Divisions on "Synoptic" & Sections of Gas Covering. Routine. Necessary fatigues.	
ADS	3rd		Routine. Necessary fatigues. Routine.	
ADS	4th		"	
ADS	5th		One N.C.O. & nine O.R. received from the Base and posted to the 1st Field Ambulance. One N.C.O. & nine O.R. detached from 1st Field Ambulance & despatched to join Base details. New Bearers being fast helped and furnished 1 Ration & necessary Trenches. 1st Troop to Supply working parties of 20 men up to day to 1st Brigade Divisional Engineers to make out plan Valley and wheels used as Main toured. Carriers wheeling & stretching cases.	
AD.S.	6th		Routine. Necessary fatigues. 2/1705 Pte. G. Brenton R.A.M.C. Divisional Train attached 1st F.A. appointed –	

WAR DIARY or INTELLIGENCE SUMMARY

Army Form C. 2118.

1st FIELD AMBULANCE, ROYAL NAVAL DIV.

Instructions regarding War Diaries and Intelligence Summaries are contained in F. S. Regs., Part II. and the Staff Manual respectively. Title pages will be prepared in manuscript.

Place	Date	Hour	Summary of Events and Information	Remarks and references to Appendices
CORBIE N/J	August 6		Provisional Lance Corporal (Unpaid)	
Do.	7		Routine heavy fatigues	
Do.	8		2 nurses officers & a Rover Sub divisions from 3rd Field Ambulance relieved section under training from 3rd Field Ambulance at the Advanced Dressing Station – relief party the same. Routine. Heavy fatigues	
Do.	9		Exploit in Ritchi, Otpen, Chérisy &c – Establishments or completed. Passed an hour after lunch.	
Do.	10		Duty. B Sub Sections on duty on the Nurses Dressing Station. Return were not able divided in occurrence in releases as to actual in the Sun without their cape. Extract from Part II Orders – the following promotions have been made & are approved to date from 7th August 1916.	
			8/3077 Corporal E Pinneter to be Acting Sergeant Clerk with pay	
			8/3246 Corporal GD Toleron " " " Lance Sergeant " "	
			8/3390 Lof Corporal J Starh " " " Corporal " "	

WAR DIARY
or
INTELLIGENCE SUMMARY

(Erase heading not required.)

Army Form C. 2118.
FIELD AMBULANCE, ROYAL NAVAL DIV.

Place	Date	Hour	Summary of Events and Information	Remarks and references to Appendices
COUP IGNY	August 10th		Ptes. R Brennan to be acting Lance Corporal with pay.	
			" S Whalley " " " " " "	
			Routine & necessary fatigues	
Do.	11th		The following Transfers to take place	
			2/3616 Corpl Kingston from C. Tent to B Tent	
			2/3488 Sick Room " B Tent to C Tent	
			2/3540 Corpl Brown " C Bearers to A Tent (Corpl Peach to Tent.)	
			2/3390 " Stark " A. Bearers to C Bearers	
			2/3361 Lance Corpl Whalley " B Tent to B Bearers	
			2/3498 " McKenzie " B Tent to B Bearers	
			2/3186 " " Noel " C Bearers to B Tent	
			2/3744 O/S J Brown " E Tent to B Bearers.	
			Griffiths from Indoor Cooking of D.O. I. S. will be handed over by Field Cashier to the mortuary orderlies as extra Share of Profits of Gardens.	
			Routine & necessary fatigues	
Do.	12th		Surgeon Schlesinger will arrange to pay a Mantelotte once weekly over 40 crops &	

Army Form C. 2118.
FIELD AMBULANCE,
ROYAL NAVAL DIV.

WAR DIARY
or
INTELLIGENCE SUMMARY.
(Erase heading not required.)

Instructions regarding War Diaries and Intelligence Summaries are contained in F. S. Regs., Part II. and the Staff Manual respectively. Title pages will be prepared in manuscript.

Place	Date	Hour	Summary of Events and Information	Remarks and references to Appendices
	August			
LOUVENCY	12th		Men into tent sub divisions & on "nursing duty". Routine nursing fatigues.	
Do.	13th		Lecture. Stopper of Carr upon a lecture to all nursing personnel in "Anti-Typ Precautions". We are also arranging to take first 20 or men in Anti-Typ. Inoculation still under performance. Lecture from Parnis under "Empire draws, Previous drains & human drains are very urgent segment. However, rotten in Exploration Fortnitain we to be renewed at S.T.O. by 9am 14th inst. Routine nursing fatigues.	
Do.	14th		Routine nursing fatigues.	
Do.	15th		Nos 1 Officer & 33 O.R. of 3rd Field ambulance returned. Personnel Bearer subdivision under training from 3rd Field ambulance as advised. Drawing stations to Bearer Relay Posts.	
Do.	16th		Routine nursing fatigues.	
Do.	17th		B Section relieved A Section at A.D.S Messin Post, C Sect Subdivn "Cherry" at M.D.S	

Army Form C. 2118.

1st FIELD AMBULANCE, ROYAL NAVAL DIV.

WAR DIARY
or
INTELLIGENCE SUMMARY.
(Erase heading not required.)

Place	Date	Hour	Summary of Events and Information	Remarks and references to Appendices
	August			
Coop16NJ	18th		Transfer - The Transfer of 3/3697 Pte W Wooley 1st Field Ambulance 63rd RN Div" to 63rd Divisional Train - Approved	
			Medical orn - Even kilopond to Indian Stores in expecting are to be refunded to viewing, even before commuter steps & a bag having specimens written out for impression of the Bn. Durning.	
190	19th		Routine - necessary fatigues.	
			Transfer. = S/21+2 Pte L.J. Pearson Div" Train act 1st to Transferred to NS 2	
			By Div Train: Grainshay 17S343 Pte W Buckingham att. TM.T from 701 coy A.S.C.	
			6/99214. Pte S. Stone att M.T. Transferred to 701 Coy A.S.C.	
Do	20th		T.1/SR/70 Acting Staffsergeant Major W Pearn proceeds for duty from 63rd RN Div Train	
Do	21		Routine - necessary fatigues	
Do	22		Routine necessary fatigues	
			Medical Board assembled av orderly Room at 11-30 am to hold a Survey on Pte L.G. Bedford 4th Bedfordshire Regt. The Board sates to consist of.	

Army Form C. 2118.

FIELD AMBULANCE,
ROYAL NAVAL DIV.

WAR DIARY
or
INTELLIGENCE SUMMARY.
(Erase heading not required.)

Place	Date	Hour	Summary of Events and Information	Remarks and references to Appendices
	August			
COURISNY	22nd		Shoeburyness Slinning. Meeting — Surgeon Walker & David Hamden R.a.m.C. Committee for disposal of Canteen Profits — Surgn Walker, Capt Hutter, Sr. McLagan	
do.	23rd		OC held P.E.? Attention drawn to standing orders re FIRES & EXPLOSIVES	
			8/3276 Sgt Murray to proceed to MONTREUIL reports to authority (authority DHQ No 233/A) for one month's attachment.	
			LEAVE the General application for leave for 8ct T.R Knowles approved & he is to leave forthwith for England warrant issued.	
			8/3372 Sergeant Tantalum returned to duty after ceasing duties Treatment at A.R.Q.U.E.S.	
			Move 1 Officer & 30 O.R. from 3rd Field Ambce relieve Beau Soir detm from 3rd field Ambce at A.D.S.	
do.	24th		Meaning fatigues	
do.	25th		Move — C Section relieved B Section at A.D.S. Leaving M.D.S. at 8 am for RIX NOULETTE	
do.	26th		Meaning fatigues —	

Army Form C. 2118

FIELD AMBULANCE,
ROYAL NAVAL DIV.

No.

WAR DIARY
or
INTELLIGENCE SUMMARY.
(Erase heading not required.)

Instructions regarding War Diaries and Intelligence Summaries are contained in F. S. Regs., Part II. and the Staff Manual respectively. Title pages will be prepared in manuscript.

Place	Date	Hour	Summary of Events and Information	Remarks and references to Appendices
COUPIGNY	August 27th		Routine. Weenary fatigues.	
DO	28th		Routine. Weenary fatigues.	
DO	29th		Above the Bearer Sub-division at A.D.S from 3rd Field Ambulance returned to Div Rec station to relieve to be sent a working party of 12 men sent from M.D.S 1st N.Z.F.A to assist in making new Bearer relay posts. Routine. Weenary fatigues.	
DO	30th		Medical Order – Evacuation of Infectious Cases – All Infectious cases are to be sent in the Care of the Field Orderlies to No 7 General Hospital MALASSISE except Enteric – Diphtheria , early Scarlet fever and Enteric fever which will be sent to C.C.S by convoy. Weenary fatigues.	
DO	31st		Routine. Weenary fatigues.	

C. F. Skevington
Staff Surgeon R.N.
OC 1st Field Ambulance
63rd R.N. Div

MEDICAL

CONFIDENTIAL

VOL. 4

1st FIELD AMBULANCE, ROYAL NAVAL DIV.
No.
Date 1 Oct/16

Sept 1916

WAR DIARY

of

1st FIELD AMBULANCE 63rd (RN) Divn

from 1st September 1916
to 30th September 1916

A.F. Fleming
STAFF SURGEON, R.N.
O.C. 1st FIELD AMBCE. R.N.D.

COMMITTEE FOR THE MEDICAL HISTORY OF THE WAR
Date 30 OCT. 1916

WAR DIARY or INTELLIGENCE SUMMARY

Army Form C. 2118.

Place	Date	Hour	Summary of Events and Information	Remarks and references to Appendices
COUTIGNY	September 1st		Joining :- 10015 Pte. J.E. BIRD and. 90/046. Pte. A. FRYER from 1st R.M. Batt. attached to field ambulance for duty. Routine - Necessary fatigues.	
DO	2nd		Routine - Necessary fatigues. Move - A Section with Surgeons WALKER and RAY-MOUAT left at 8 am to relieve C Section at A.D.S. 6 men from C Section to remain behind at A.D.S. for work our Bearer Relay post. B. Section took over work on hands at M.D.S.	
DO	3rd		Routine - Necessary fatigues. The following Officers & N.C.O's detailed to attend a course of Instruction at the Divisional Gas School - BOYEFFLES - To appear at 6 pm on 7.9.16. - Capt. CRAIG - Sergt FERGUSON. Corpl. MARTIN. Corp TILLEY. Lee Corp. SIMPSON	
DO	4th		Routine - Necessary fatigues. The under mentioned N.C.O "acting" are approved for confirmation to Substantive Rank to date from 1st Sept, 1916.	

WAR DIARY or INTELLIGENCE SUMMARY

Army Form C. 2118.

(Erase heading not required.)

Place	Date	Hour	Summary of Events and Information	Remarks and references to Appendices
COUDRIGNY	September 4th		S/3077 acting Sergt E. BROOKE. S/3946 acting Lance Corpl TOLSON. S/3390 acting Corporal J.A. STARK. S/3827 acting Lance Corpl R. EMMERSON. S/3361 acting Lance Corpl B. WHALLEY.	
DO	5th		MEDICAL ORDER Attention drawn to the proper filling in & signing by Medical Officers of Field Service Medical Cards. DISPOSAL OF Pte. BIRD and Pte FRYER reported 1st R.M. Base from this Ambulance - authority Routine Order 569. Routine - necessary fatigues.	
DO	6th		MEDICAL ORDER - Greatest care to be exercised that no sketches be drawn up from fires or Beacon Posts which may be in enemy posts to position. Routine - necessary fatigues.	
DO	7th		Routine - necessary fatigues.	
DO	8th		Routine - necessary fatigues.	
DO	9th		The Field Ambulance was inspected by Director General Medical Services in France British Armies - Sir A.T. Sloggett. He inspected wards, outpatient, Sanitary arrangements, Grounds & Transport.	

WAR DIARY
or
INTELLIGENCE SUMMARY.
(Erase heading not required.)

Army Form C. 2118.

Place	Date	Hour	Summary of Events and Information	Remarks and references to Appendices
Couginy	Sept 8th		The Director General was accompanied by Surgeon General Pike, P.M. Army and Col. Meek Rams, 18 Corps. The A.D.M.S. 63rd Div was also present. The Director General expressed himself as pleased with the arrangements made & the working of the Ambulance	
Do.	9th		MOs B. Sections deployed and 5 bearer sections taken to cross roads D.59 b.9.E. Routine bearing parties	
Do.	10th		Major B. Section left M.D.S. at 9 am to relieve A section as A.D.S. 6 men from A. Section to be left at A.D.S. for purp of working parties at new bearer relay post. Surgeon ADAM and Corpl CRAIG left unit. B. Section & C. Section both on Hospital duties at M.D.S.	
Do.	11th		Routine other ranks moved to higher reserve warning them to be continue information of the wounds under than change during their watch on duty. Prospects. Pickets – On transport lines. 45 other wounds of limes to Sudden officers during the night	
Do.	12th		Routine bearing fatigues.	

WAR DIARY or INTELLIGENCE SUMMARY.

Army Form C. 2118.

(Erase heading not required.)

Instructions regarding War Diaries and Intelligence Summaries are contained in F. S. Regs., Part II. and the Staff Manual respectively. Title pages will be prepared in manuscript.

Place	Date	Hour	Summary of Events and Information	Remarks and references to Appendices
COUPIGNY	Sept. 13th		Routine. Necessary fatigues	
DO	14th		Routine. Necessary fatigues. Medical order - Officers when being changed about are to notify its orderly room immediately giving new address and name forward.	
DO	15th		Routine. Necessary fatigues	
DO	16th		Army order No 9257/M read out on parade. Attached Surgeon E.J. Schlesinger attached for duty, at the 18th C.C.S and left today to take up his new appointment. (Authority IV Corps D.D.M.S)	
DO	17th		Surgn Kay Menon to inspect works. Early Mass at 11.30 am and to make an weekly inventory inspection. Have been forces feeling it.	
DO	18th		Move C. Section witdraw by a Frehim B Section at A.D.S. Move the 49th Field Ambulance takes over the Main Dressing Station from today	

WAR DIARY
or
INTELLIGENCE SUMMARY.
(Erase heading not required.)

Army Form C. 2118.

Place	Date	Hour	Summary of Events and Information	Remarks and references to Appendices
COUPIGNY	Sept. 18th		Move the 48th Field Ambulance to take over the A.D.S. at AIX-NOULETTE today. Surgeon COX INGS and 4 O.R. left last evening for Q.19.D.6.1 (Ref map 36 B J. (FRESNICOURT) to take over Dressing Station there from 48th Field Ambulance and arrange for feeding up. Surplus stores returns at M.D.S. and A.D.S. and Bearer Posts to be handed over to our Relief & receipts obtained. Transport for B Section down to A.D.S. to bring back B Section Motor Ambulance Stores when B Section moves out. B Section at A.D.S. given orders to leave direct for Q.19.D.6.1 when relieved at Bearer Post & A.D.S. by 48th Field Ambulance. TRANSPORT: Surgeon WALKER Escort as Transport Officer and Lt. WILLIAMS as Camp Transport Officer. Transport & Personnel fall in ready to move off about 2.45 p.m.	See No. 1 July 30.
		3 p.m.	Marched off from CUPIGNY for FRESNICOURT (Q.19.D.6.1) Refmap 36 B	
FRESNICOURT		4.25 p.m.	Arrived at FRESNICOURT with A & C Sections & Transport & Personnel and	

WAR DIARY or INTELLIGENCE SUMMARY.

(Erase heading not required.)

Army Form C. 2118.

Place	Date	Hour	Summary of Events and Information	Remarks and references to Appendices
FRESNICOURT	18th	4.30	Took over from 46th Field Ambulance. Transfer of Patients – All cases not fit for duty in 48 hours sent to C.C.S. Cases fit for duty within 48 hours to accompany ambulance motor march. Other cases & sedan transferred to 49 Field Ambulance.	
FRESNICOURT	19th		A Section taken on duty in wards. B Section arrived at 11 am with transport & particulars of Gores from A.D.S. & Reserve Post after turning over to pany, from 46th Field Ambulance including stores. Stores to be arranged in sections ready for immediate move. S/3972 Pte S. BEASLEY to report to R.T.O. BARLIN for movement order. Leave here 9.30 am. arrived in London to report personally to War Office and will proceed to join O.T.C. (Australia) War Office Telegram (CR. No 36484/S/B).	
Do.	20th		Patients transferred to 6 General Section Clinic from Hornet & Brechin Boats at HERMIN & Horse ambulance for such of Hutson & Hurche Railway Magnicourt & Monchy Breton	
Do.	21st		Sedan Case to be sent to 2nd F.A. Routine. Necessary telegram	
Do.	22nd		Work on Horse Standings for units to be commenced. Reinforcements from 2.30 am to 11.45 am Horse ambulances to collect sick slack from Hornet & Brechin Boats at HERMIN & Horse ambulances for such of Hutson & Hurche Railway Magnicourt & Monchy Breton	

Army Form C. 2118.

WAR DIARY
or
INTELLIGENCE SUMMARY.
(Erase heading not required.)

Place	Date	Hour	Summary of Events and Information	Remarks and references to Appendices
FRESNICOURT	Sept. 23rd		Route march – Coys B Section left at 9.30 am for route march. Car Helmer dried at 1-30 pm for all not engaged on duty.	
Do.	24th		Routine necessary fatigues. Surgeon RITCHIE left for 1st R.M. Boat Temporarily attached probably. Signal 2.	
Do.	25th		Instruction as per Jas. School – Surgeon Kay MOVAT, Surgeon E.D. COX. Stretcher W.M.S.H, Sergt. HILSHAW, Sergt. SWAIN, Corpl NELSON, Corpl STARK, Lce Corpl HILL to be leave at 9 am from listing for course of Instruction at above School. Instruction to finish on Septr 26th pm. B. Section Stretcher drill from 8.30 am to day. 1st Field Ambulance to take on again Waterment of Sections. 2nd Field Ambulance to hamper all details to 1st F.A. Lautenay. Messages from Districts J. & Surgeon Chandre Commenced for the Population Clothing Sedden Care to renew had been required by Personnel. Personnel drawn into billets & no other huts.	Signal No 3
Do.	26th		Route march – From 10 am to 12.30 pm. Returne Field Day Parading for horse.	
Do.	27th		Patients moved into Huts about 20 of Same down line to REBREUVE. Captain Moore attended Same time.	

Army Form C. 2118.

WAR DIARY
or
INTELLIGENCE SUMMARY.
(Erase heading not required.)

Place	Date	Hour	Summary of Events and Information	Remarks and references to Appendices
FRESNICOURT	September 27th		Routine Inspection Philipos. Philip - The medical officer went for duty, was made No 2 Reserve Park. OLHAIN at 9-30 am each day to see the sick during the absence in leave of the medical officer of the unit.	
Do.	29th		Field Day Operations - Established a dressing station at PREVILLERS. and an Advanced Dressing Station at HERLIN LE VERT. Section A left camp at 6 am for their villages & were in position by 9. am. Surgn WALKER in charge of A Section established with R.A.P. of 169th Inf. Brigade after establishing an advanced dressing station at HERLIN LE VERT. Transport 2 Motor Ambulances 1 Horse Ambulance 1 S.S. wagon 1 water cart 1 Motor cyclist 1 Cyclist 2 Wheeled Stretcher Carriers. Store Pack of Sections M.S.T. Stores. Lieut Hamlin and Dr. took main dressing station. Operations finished at 2 p.m. and Sections returned to camp at 4.15 p.m.	

WAR DIARY
or
INTELLIGENCE SUMMARY.

Army Form C. 2118.

Place	Date	Hour	Summary of Events and Information	Remarks and references to Appendices
FRESNICOURT	Sept. 28th		Routine - heavy fatigues	
do	30th		Re inclusion by Officers of sick dinners. Men now to carry extra unnecessary kit in their packs. Officers to attempt to send their surplus kit to England as soon as possible. Routine - heavy fatigues	

C. L. Fleming
A/Capt R.A.M.C.
O.C. 1st Field Ambulance
63rd Rn Div.

"A" Form.
MESSAGES AND SIGNALS.
Army Form C. 2121.

TO: O C 1st F A

Sender's Number: O.O.7
Day of Month: 17-9-16
AAA

Your F.A will move to FRESNICOURT on 18/19th of Sept: being relieved on the 18th AAA Detailed instructions concerning movement later and secret instructions concerning movement of stores herewith AAA

From: Medical
Place: Nœux
Time: 9.35 am

(Sgd) E J Finch ?/Lt

"A" Form.
Army Form C. 2121.
MESSAGES AND SIGNALS.

TO O.C. 1st F.A.

Sender's Number: 25/13
Day of Month: 23.9.16
AAA

Please detail a naval medical Officer to join up with 1st R.M. Battn on the evening of the 24th inst. aaa Surgn EDYKYN 1st R.M. will proceed on leave on the morning of the 25th aaa Location of 1st R.M. — DIEVAL aaa Please report name of M.O. sent aaa

From: Medical
Place: Naval
Time: 8 pm

(Sd) E.J. Finch Whipp

"A" Form.
MESSAGES AND SIGNALS.

Army Form C. 2121.

TO: O C 1st Fd Amb C

Sender's Number: F883
Day of Month: 23.9.16
AAA

It will be necessary for you to take over the Scabies cases again as no accommodation can be found for 2nd FA suitable for treating patients in and they must move to-morrow. You will have either to get another hut lent you or clear out the hut occupied by your personnel & put them under canvas. Stanford will send 3 baths with the Scabies patients tomorrow morning AAA

From: Medical
Place: Naval
Time: 5.0pm

Sgd E J Finch Lt Surg.

MEDICAL.

CONFIDENTIAL
VOLUME 5.

WAR DIARY

of

1st FIELD AMBULANCE of 63rd (RN) DIVISION.

FROM 1st OCTOBER 1916

To 31st OCTOBER 1916

A.F. Hennessy
STAFF SURGEON, R.N.
O.O. 1st FIELD AMBCE. R.N.D.

WAR DIARY or INTELLIGENCE SUMMARY.

Army Form C. 2118.

Vol 5

Place	Date	Hour	Summary of Events and Information	Remarks and references to Appendices
FRESNICOURT	October			
	1st		Routine - training fatigues	
do.	2nd		Leave S/3145 Pte. F.W. FORD proceeded on 10 days leave to England. Hospital duties - C Tent Subsection take over duties from B Tent Subsection at 9.30 a.m.	
			Route march - Surgeon Key, Horan, in charge commencing at 9.30 a.m. for Corps B. Sections	
do.	3rd		Military Officers Rounds - until further notice will be at 9 p.m. instead of 9.30 a.m. In that's Lieut. J.P. BROWN. Rams porter from 49th Field Ambulance for duty with 1st Field Ambulance.	
			Part II. The undermentioned promotions are approved to date 1st September 1916. S/3663 Pte. E. BARLOW to Corpl Clerk with pay & posted to B Tent. S/8304 Sergt. N. ELLIOTT to Staff Sergeant with pay.	
			MOVE - The Transport including Motor ambulances, Bicycles, wheeled Stretcher Carriers, Officers grooms & horses left at 8 a.m. for CANETTEMONT (Ref. map LENS II). Where they were billetted for night of 3rd & 4th. From CANETTEMONT they will leave further	(See Copy of Operation Orders attached (No.1)

WAR DIARY or INTELLIGENCE SUMMARY

Army Form C. 2118.

Place	Date	Hour	Summary of Events and Information	Remarks and references to Appendices
FRESNICOURT	Oct. 3rd		Orders as to 15. Horse Major moved. Sleigh Car of Sick will go in motor ambulances. Sleigh will be transferred 15. at ESTRÉE, CAUCHIE. Other cars to C.C.S. Surgeon WALKER was in charge of transport. LIEUT HAMELIN was to write Motor Ambulances & Sick. Supply wagons of Intendance by road will draw supplies in Rieulis in the evening of 3rd for Consumption on 4th. Personnel of Field Ambulance will leave in 3 detachments each comprising ½ 2 Officers & 47 O.R. for entraining station LIGNY Sʳ FLUCHEL. 1 detachment will leave camp at motorphi 3ᵐ write O.R. to Entrainmente Supervision, & 47 O.R. They are to the entrainstation by 6 am 4.10.16. 2nd detachment with Surgeon Adam Capt Craig & 48 O.R. leave camp at 5·30 am on 4ᵗʰ They are to the ar-station by 1 am train depart. 9.27 am 3rd detachment — with Surgeon King - Monat Surgeon Coxe & 48 O.R. leave Camp at 11 am on 4ᵗʰ to be at Station by 6.30 pm or ar.train depart. 9.29 pm The Route to be followed from FRESNICOURT will be via CAUCOURT, BÉTHONSART, VILLERS, BRULIN.	

WAR DIARY
or
INTELLIGENCE SUMMARY.

Army Form C. 2118.

Place	Date	Hour	Summary of Events and Information	Remarks and references to Appendices
FRESNICOURT	Sept 3rd		TINQUES then along ST POL road to entraining station at LIGNY FLOCHEL	
DO	4th	AM	Had ambulance on the march	
		PM	About 1st detachment arrived 6.30am FOREVILLE	
FOREVILLE	5th		2nd & 3rd detachments arrived	
			Took over hospital huts etc from 6th London Field Ambulance. Routine - Cleaning up hospital.	
DO	6th		Transport arrived A.M. Torking LIEUT J.P.BROWN R.A.M.C to B leaves Tents. Duty starts for huts. Convoy to be at officers stationed by 6 am daily. Hospital huts etc. cleaned up. Separate started. Surgeon A.D.M.S inspected present sanitation & stated sanitary latrines, incinerators & cook-houses. 6 sections continued hospital duties.	
DO	7th		Preparations began for to build & hospital huttings to be Severe cases to be transferred by 5 no F.A at CLAIR FAYE.	
			Medical Officers to be drawn from 16 Advanced Medical Stores Depot BEAUVAL	
RD	8th		Leave to rest camps. The following O.R left today for rest camp at AULT Pte Derrick J.P Train, Stirland, Shirbson, Humphries, Smith J. & Reedy. J	

WAR DIARY
INTELLIGENCE SUMMARY

Army Form C. 2118.

Place	Date	Hour	Summary of Events and Information	Remarks and references to Appendices
FRICOURT	October 8th		Took over A.D.S. Bernes Posts from 5th Field Ambulance at RED HOUSE. MAILLY MAILLET (map ref Sheet 57D. O.1.D.3.3.) hereby equipment down also. move to be completed by 12 noon. Party left M.D.S. at 7.45. Surgeon WALKER in charge. Surgeon Ritchie and BROWN to commence duty. 2 Squads of men from A.S.C. mess the purpose of fuel ambulance carriages from Puchevilles. This now serving in expected trenches to new lines now established. Move completed.	
Do	9th	11.30 am	Lieut. Surgeon BARNES returned on leave from 19.10.16 to 20.10.16.	
			Posting. Surgeon COX left for duty with horse Batt. taken up Duty. A few Sec. ans take on duties in Hospital at E.B.D. from E Tent. Routine - necessary fatigues	
Do	10th		Routine necessary fatigues	
Do	11th		Joining - 8/3120 Qr. F. GREENROY.D. Private from Div Supernt Parties to E Reserve	

T.134. Wt. W708-776. 500000. 4/15. Sir J. C. & S.

WAR DIARY
or
INTELLIGENCE SUMMARY.
(Erase heading not required.)

Army Form C. 2118.

Place	Date	Hour	Summary of Events and Information	Remarks and references to Appendices
FORCEVILLE	11th		TRANSFER - S/303, Pte. W. BOWERS transferred from C Section to B Section for duty.	
DO.	12th		Medical Officer - Before setting over - Message to be sent to E.M.O. at C.C.S. ACHEUX notifying number visiting cases daily. Returned to send him by 1 horse ambulance cars for C.C.S. to leave M.D.S. in horse ambulance daily at 8 a.m. & 5 p.m. Turn over to E.M.O. at C.C.S. ACHEUX on arrival. Named will be accompanying cases.	
			Routine necessary [stores?]	
DO.	13th			
DO.	14th		Relief the Squad from A/3 or horses to relieve similar numbers Squad at A/S. Park to leave at 7.30 a.m. for D.H.Q. Addition the SAFIELD Ambulance (3rd Divn) arrived at FORCEVILLE. They will be billeted in village. Their Sub-Chief will assist at Hospital. FORCEVILLE. Col WRIGHT R.A.M.C. & Lieut Andrew will be in charge & make necessary arrangements for establishing & evacuating of wounded coming thro' from A.D.S. Combined M.D.S. if this is not Ambulance 63rd Div & 8th Field Ambulance 3rd Divn will be at FORCEVILLE All sick from 3rd Divn will be evacuated by 8th F.A.	

WAR DIARY or INTELLIGENCE SUMMARY.

Army Form C. 2118.

Place	Date	Hour	Summary of Events and Information	Remarks and references to Appendices
FOREEVILLE	15th		Relief of our Squad from W.B & hernion to relieve Dunlap Squad at A.D.S. Party leave M.D.S at 7.30 a.m	
Do.	16th		Routine. Necessary fatigues.	
Do.	17th		Relief. B Tent Sub division taken over Inspected duties from A Tent Sub div at 8.30 a.m.	
Do.	18th	MOVE	Routine necessary fatigues. A.D.S. at MAILLY-MAILLET turned over to study field Amble. Field Ambulance moved from FOREEVILLE to VARENNES & took over from 6th Field Ambulance	S.C. Capt G. Spalding Gun battery (No 2)
VARENNES		p.m	Field Ambulance arrived at 2.30 p.m. Proceed to establish a dressing station for reception of wounded. Accommodation for patients nearby in huts + for about 450.	
Do.	19th		The following have joined from Base (Rouen) 74189 Pte H WOODHOUSE 21,328 Pte T WATSON, 76302 Pte H WOOD, 24776 Pte S WALKER	
Do.	20th		The following rejoined from C.C.S 8/3361 Pte S BALL 8/3989 J WINTERBOTTOM posting LIEUT J G BROWN came at Beaurs. 95 H PILKINGTON at Beaurs from C Beaurs. Pts WALKER, WOOD, WATSON, WOODHOUSE & B Keening	

WAR DIARY
INTELLIGENCE SUMMARY

Army Form C. 2118.

Place	Date	Hour	Summary of Events and Information	Remarks and references to Appendices
VARENNES	Sept 20th		Huts repaired for reception of wounded. Dressing Tt. camp. Operating & dressing rooms prepared & dressings for 1000 patients ordered. Dressings & rations indented for & received	
Do	21		Lieut S/303 P.S.W. BOWERS proceeded on leave to England to return from Southampton on 31st inst. Lieutenant Surg Maher REWCASTLE 2 NCOs & 2 OR from A.P.S. Leave ripe for A.D.S. at MESNIL is seen trenches & north devastation supervised. Lieut Brown 2 NCOs & 2 OR from A.B.S. Bearers ripe for A.D.S. at Cothrun to bearer trench devastation for wounded. Interchange between two parties is to arranged	
Do			Morning — Pts D.L.E.S. Div. Train attached. Issued medical supplies from R.A.M. for duty	
Do	22nd		Routine necessary fatigues. Preparing Camp for wounded	
Do	23rd		Duty, 6 tent H.orrh. duties from B Sant. Subsection detached duty. 10 tent D.R.s proceed to 44 C.C.S. Puchsvillers for detached duty	
Do	24th		Army D.S. return to M.D.S. Routine necessary fatigues Party proceed	

WAR DIARY
or
INTELLIGENCE SUMMARY.

Army Form C. 2118.

Place	Date	Hour	Summary of Events and Information	Remarks and references to Appendices
VARENNES	Dec 25th		Attached Corps. Lieut D H DANIELS R.A.M.C S.N.Co.s & 31 P[rivate]s of 48th Field Amble Capt. H.R SOUPER R.A.M.C. 49th Field Amble Capt. H.N. STAFFORD R.A.M.C 50th Field Ambles joined for temp duty A Combined Main Dressing Station for B.3rd Div & 37th Div will be established at VARENNES for Reception & Forwarding Div'l Sick Amble 49th Fd Div in charge. Medical Arrangements made for Bernburg M.D.S From Rations. All Bearer N.C.O's Men are to ensure that their iron Rations are Complete.	Copy attached Medical Arrangements
DO.	26th		Routine. Necessary Fatigues Brazier, Water fetched up in turn if Stoves covered be retained	
DO	27th		Joining. 9/3325 Pte A GRIEVES & 9/3194 Pte C MAUNDRELL joined Yesterday from Base, in former in orders to B Tenn, the Latta to C Bearen	
			Return to duty from leave — Sergt Major A.W BARNES	
DO	28th		Routine — Necessary Fatigues —	

WAR DIARY
INTELLIGENCE SUMMARY

Army Form C. 2118.

Place	Date	Hour	Summary of Events and Information	Remarks and references to Appendices
VARENNES	Oct. 29		Routine necessary fatigues. Dispersed - 74169 Pte H. WOODHOUSE. Rank 24776 Pte S. WALKER Rank 76302 Pte H WOOD Rank 21528 Pte T. WATSON Rank left for duty with 142 Field Ambulance (continued absent)	
do.	30th		Duty. A Tent Subdivision relieved E Tent Subdivision in Hospital Routine - necessary fatigues	
do.	31st		Move Capt SOUPER Rank 50th Field Ambulance Capt STAFFORD Rank 46th Field Ambulance and LIEUT. DANIELS Rank 46th Field Ambulance and 39 O.R. from 46 Field Ambulance left to return to their respective units (withdrawn from 37th Divn.)	

A.F. Fleming
Staff Surgeon R.N.
O.C. 1st Field Ambulance
63rd Div. R.N.D.

Copy Secret   Headquarters
          ①   63 (RN) Divⁿ
                      2 Oct. 1916

Extract from 63 (RN) Divⁿ Medical Unit
Operation Order No 8.

Para 2. Field Ambulances will, as regards vehicles and mounted personnel, be ready for an early start tomorrow and will be billeted on the night 3rd/4th in the FREVENT-REKREUVIETTE area, (1st dropping place)

                 Sgd. E. J. Finch
                      Fleet Surgeon RN &
                      ADMS 63 (RN) D.

Copy   3rd Oct. 1916

       Extract
In continuation of
63 (RN) Divⁿ Medical Unit
    Operation Order No 8.

Para 3. The detachments of 1st Field Amble ᵒᶠ from FRESNICOURT will march via SAUCOURT, BETHONSART, VILLIERS BOURIN, TINQUES and will arrive at entraining station 1¼ hours before their respective trains start.

                 Sgd. E. J. Finch
                      Fleet Surgeon RN &
                      ADMS 63 (RN) Divⁿ

Copy. Secret.   (2)

                                Hd Quarters
                                63 (RN) Divn
                                18-10-16

Extract from 63 (RN) Division
        Medical Unit
Operation Order No 12.   Map Reference
                          Sheet 57 D.

Para 2. No 1 Field Ambulance will take over the Dressing Station at VARENNES from No 6 Field Ambulance 2nd Division, on the afternoon of the 18th.

                        Sgd   F. Casement Capt. RAMC.
                        for   Fleet Surgeon RN. and
                              ADMS. 63 (RN) Divn

Medical Arrangements

Combined Main Dressing Station of the 1st Field Ambulance 63 (RN) Div & the 48th Field Ambulance, 37th Div.

P.25 D.2 6 (Map reference 57.D)

Bringing in of Wounded

Ambulance cars from 63rd Div & probably 37th Div will convey wounded from A.D.S" to VARENNES and stop at entrance to hospital. (See attached map of hospital). A fatigue party will be in readiness to carry stretchers from cars along to Reception Tents. If Dressing Room is full, the wounded whilst waiting will be given hot drinks (Bovril, Soups, Tea) and sandwiches. Very urgent cases will be brought direct into Dressing Room.

Pack Store

At entrance to hospital for receiving kit, and issuing blankets & stretchers to Amb'ce Cars as they arrive from ADS.

Dressing Room & Operating Room

As wounded are brought into Dressing Room their particulars are taken on A.F. 3210, and a serial number given each patient & from that A.F.W. 3118 will be made out. This when completed will be attached to patient & also serial number. Anti-Tetanic Serum will be given to each patient. In Dressing Room & Operating Room 4 Tables will be available, the less serious & walking cases being dressed in Dressing Room, the serious cases in Operating Room. When patients are dressed they are carried (in direction of arrow, see map) in M.A.C. cars if available and sent to 4th or 11th CCS. If cars are not available patients are brought into huts to await convoy.

Clerking Arrangements

Two Clerks from 63rd & 37th Divisions will be on duty in Dressing Room where each will make out A.F.W. 3210 & A.F.W. 3118 for his respective Division. Other formations will be attended to as they arrive.

By arrangements with 4th & 11th CCS a red cross will be put on an A.F.W. 3118 to show that this case will not require dressing for 24 hours. Cases sent to CCS which do not have a red cross on A.F.W. 3118 will require further treatment at CCS.

A.F.W. 3210 when filled in will be sent to Orderly Room the A.F.W. 3210 of 63 (RN) Div placed in a separate compartment of a box marked 63 (RN) Div and those of 37th Div placed in a compartment marked 37th Div. Other formations also in a separate compartment. In Orderly Room 2 Clerks from 63rd & 37th Divisions will make out from A.F.W. 3210 the A.& D. Book of their own Division & also A.F. 36. There will be a separate A.& D. Book for Officers & also for German Wounded. A separate A.F. 36 will be made out for German Wounded. There will be an N.C.O. at exit (see map) whose duty will be to check all cases that pass out for M.A.C. & take off serial number from A.F.W. 3118 & return it to Orderly Room thus ensuring a check on all evacuations.

Personnel

The 1st Field Ambulance will supply 3 Medical Officers.

Evacuation Duties	1 Staff Sergt or Sergt	
Checkers & Stretcher Stokers	1 N.C.O.	1 PTE
Clerks	2 N.C.Os	2 PTES
Dressers		8 PTES
General Duty (Feeders &c)		2 PTES
Bearers	1 N.C.O.	8 PTES
Cooks		4 PTES
Sanitary Duties		3 PTES
Police Duties		2 PTES
Burial Duties		1 PTE
TOTAL	5 N.C.Os	31 PTES

The 48th Field Ambulance will provide a similar party.

Cooking

The Cooking arrangements will be under the Q.M. of the 1st Field Ambulance who has orders to have Soups, Bovril, Tea, Cocoa, Ham Sandwiches going day + night.

A Corporal Cook from 1st Field Amb^{ce} will be in charge of Cook house.

It is hoped that fatigue parties for stretcher work + sanitary duties will be provided from 63 Div, composed of P.B. men, Convalescents etc & that 37th Div will provide a similar party. 12 P^{tes} + 2 N.C.O^s would be sufficient from each Division.

Burials

A Pte or N.C.O. will be told off for this duty who will make arrangements with grave attendant for burial at VARENNES British Cemetary. P. 25 A 2 3. (MAP 57 D) and attach A.F.W. 337.1 to each grave. The Chaplain of each denomination will be notified in ample time.

Personal Effects of Dead

These will be sealed + sent to D.A.G. BASE. Personal effects from A.D.S^s will be sealed + sent to M.D.S. VARENNES.

Kits

Steel helmets, rifles + respirators will be kept in Pack Store + D.A.D.O.S. Div will provide transport for them.

Casualty List of Each Division

will be kept from a specified hour to a specified hour (as per attached copy). This will ensure a rapid estimate of Casualties occurring in Brigades of each Division.

Shell Shock Cases

All Shell Shock cases will be seen by O.C. Main Dressing Station who will determine cases that should be sent to 2 Field Amb^{ce} CLAIRFAYE or sent to C.C.S.

A J Henry
Staff Surgeon R.N.
O.C. 1st Field Amb^{ce}

1st FIELD AMBULANCE, ROYAL NAVAL DIV.
Date 25.10.16

63rd (RN) Division. Casualties. Divisional Troops.
9 a.m. to 9 p.m. October 1916.

	WOUNDED.	TOTAL.	DIED OF WOUNDS.	TOTAL.
H.Q. 63rd Divl Engrs				
No 1 Coy do				
No 2 Coy do				
No 3 Coy do				
H.Q. Divl TRAIN.				
Divl TRAIN				
1st Fd AMBce				
2nd Fd AMBce				
3rd Fd AMBce				
14th Worcester Regt				
H.Q. Divl ARTILLERY.				
315 Bde R.F.A. "A" Batty				
do — "B" "				
do — "C" "				
do — "D" "				
317th Bde R.F.A. "A" Batty				
do — "B" "				
do — "C" "				
do — "D" "				
223 Bde R.F.A. "A" Batty				
do — "B" "				
do — "C" "				
do — "D" "				
63rd Div Am Col R.F.A.				

1st FIELD AMBULANCE, ROYAL NAVAL DIV.

63rd (RN) Division Casualties, Infantry Brigades.
9 a.m. to 9 a.m. October 1916.

	WOUNDED	TOTAL	DIED OF WOUNDS	TOTAL
188th Brigade				
1st RM Battn				
2nd RM Battn				
Howe Battn				
Anson Battn				
188 M.G.Coy				
188 T.M.Batty				
189th Brigade				
Drake Battn				
Hawke Battn				
Hood Battn				
Nelson Battn				
189th M.G.Coy				
189 T.M.Batty				
190th Brigade				
1st H.A.C.				
4th Royal Fusiliers				
7th Bedford Regt				
10 Royal Dublin Fus				
190th M.G.Coy				
190 T.M.Batty				

1st FIELD AMBULANCE, ROYAL NAVAL DIV.
No.
Date

140/862

63rd Div

1st R.N.D. Field Ambulance

Nov 1916

COMMITTEE FOR THE
MEDICAL HISTORY OF THE WAR
Date -3 JAN. 1917

MEDICAL

CONFIDENTIAL.
VOLUME 6.

Vol 6

WAR DIARY

of

1st FIELD AMBULANCE 63 (R.N.) Divn.

FROM   1st NOVEMBER 1916

TO   30th NOVEMBER 1916.

Army Form C. 2118.

WAR DIARY
or
INTELLIGENCE SUMMARY.
(Erase heading not required.)

Place	Date	Hour	Summary of Events and Information	Remarks and references to Appendices
VARENNES	Nov 1st		Attention called in orders to Slackness in dress & Saluting	
"	2nd		3.333 Sergt H Swift M.T. was reported yesterday for duty	
			M S/309 Corpl W Cockroft M.T. ad returned to 70 1 Brigade	
"	3rd		Routine. Inventory fatigues	
"	4th		Joined S/3327 Pte H.E at Hd. Qrs. S/3159 Pte J Allen S/3089 Pte H Worsley	
			Joined from base	
			M/2 149149 Pte C Douglas M.T. are posted from 63rd Divl	
			Supply Column	
"	5th		Qrtly Qtr Mstr Allen & Worsley to B Barriers	
"	6th		Routine Inventory fatigues	
"	7th		Routine Inventory fatigues	
			M/Sgt B Seaton taken on Strength dated from Aug 27th	
"	8th		Routine. Inventory fatigues	
"	9th		" Inventory fatigues	
"	9th		Extract from Army Routine orders (S/M/16) Damage to Trees	
			communicated to all Concerned	

WAR DIARY
or
INTELLIGENCE SUMMARY.
(Erase heading not required.)

Army Form C. 2118.

Place	Date	Hour	Summary of Events and Information	Remarks and references to Appendices
VARENNES	Nov 8/10/16		Journey. S/8050 Pte (A/J) COLLINSON S/3119 Cpl F. FITTON Journey Returned from Base and were posted to B Beavers to bed at 1.30 pm on dressing gown to Cornet of Nursing No 24443 Ford Ambulance Car wheels Returned on 8/10/16	
			Numbers - Present Sergts J. WALKER, Macleod-Sergt/Acting MOURT Lieut HAMELIN	
			Routine - Nursery Patigues	
AD	11:45 am		Montreuil C Bearer Cpl. Brown y-y left at 10.30 am for	
DS	12:45		ENGLEBELMER. B Bearers (Surg Ritchie) left at 8 pm for MESNIL C. Bearers (Surg Worthing) left at 2.30 pm for COOKERS	
			Each Officer N.C.O & O.R. Stacey 2 days rations, bread, Iron Rations and A & D Tribes Dress - overcoats, macintosh sheets, 2 Respirators, Steel helmets 2 pair socks	

Army Form C. 2118.

WAR DIARY
or
INTELLIGENCE SUMMARY.
(Erase heading not required.)

Instructions regarding War Diaries and Intelligence Summaries are contained in F. S. Regs., Part II. and the Staff Manual respectively. Title pages will be prepared in manuscript.

Place	Date	Hour	Summary of Events and Information	Remarks and references to Appendices
	Nov.			
VARENNES	12		Medical Equipment. Each H.Q. & Surgical Haversack, & Haversacks with three dressings per bed drawing, dressing posts for wounded. The remainder of Bearer hd. Qrs. in Pack-Sadn.	
Do.	13th		From 6 am today all wounded Coming into Bouland Main Dressing Station will be given a Cereal Number. New A.D. Station Brit's Casualty Lists made out from 6 am to 5 pm & from 5 pm to 6 am. Daily Stats. made out at 12 noon daily. & A.F. 36 rendered daily to Dons of other Divisions. Separate A.D. Book kept of all Casualties for D. Dons V Corps. Lt. DANIELS 4/6th Suff. Amber & 3 Nursing orderlies arrived for duty. Capt AUSTIN 4th PONTOON Sec. Lieut Clark R.A.M.C. attached for duty.	
Do.	14th		Patients arrived from A.D.S's at COURS & MESNIL. Received A.T. given each patient. Patients evacuated to C.C.S at VARENNES.	
Do.	15th		Received Re-dressing & evacuating patients to C.C.S.	

Army Form C. 2118.

WAR DIARY
or
INTELLIGENCE SUMMARY.
(Erase heading not required.)

Instructions regarding War Diaries and Intelligence Summaries are contained in F. S. Regs., Part II. and the Staff Manual respectively. Title pages will be prepared in manuscript.

Place	Date	Hour	Summary of Events and Information	Remarks and references to Appendices
WARENNES	Nov 15th		Receiving, retaining & evacuating patients & Sg.	
Au	16		" " " "	
Av.	17th		January. Pte OATES BAINFORTH. R.LEE joined Unit from Base	
			May. 1st Field Ambulance left air 12 noon for BEAUVAL Burying party left air 10.45 am Surplus Stores handed over to relieving Field Ambulance 148 copies annex/ Red Cross Stores handed over to 148th Field Ambulance also all Surplus rations & medical comforts	(1)
			List of Casualties. 63. R.N. Div.	
			Officers O Ranks
			63 973
			6 143
			4 109
			73 1225
			Other Ranks
			German Prisoner.	
BEAUVAL	17th 5-45 pm		Arrived BEAUVAL 5.45 pm billeted for night.	

Army Form C. 2118.

WAR DIARY
or
INTELLIGENCE SUMMARY.
(Erase heading not required.)

Place	Date	Hour	Summary of Events and Information	Remarks and references to Appendices
BEAUVAL	18th	7/10 am	Left BEAUVAL for AUTHEUX	(2)
AUTHEUX	18th	2 pm	arrived AUTHEUX. attached to 185th Inf Bde for march.	
AUTHEUX	19th		Orders given re march discipline field ambulance tents at AUTHEUX.	
AUTHEUX	19th		Joining T/Capt. D. MATTHEW, T/Capt. E. P. TIMMS, T/Capt W. TOPP with EAGLES T/Capt: H. F. GIBSON. T/Capt W. F. H. HAMILTON attached for camp duty with 1st Lines Ambce (as above) Arrived 63rd "MOrs].	
AUTHEUX	20th	9 am	first Agramass lectures	
AUTHEUX	21st	11 am	Left for VACQUERIE (BERNAVILLES) ar 11 am	(3)
VACQUERIE		2 pm	arrived at VACQUERIE ar 2 pm	
VACQUERIE	21st	9 am	Left for YVRENCH.	(4)
YVRENCH	21st	1.45 pm	arrived YVRENCH	
YVRENCH	22nd	10 am	Left YVRENCH for FONTAINE-SUR-MAYE	(5)
FONTAINE-SUR-MAYE	22nd	12.30 pm	arrived FONTAINE-SUR-MAYE	
	23rd	10 am	Left for NOUVION-EN-PONTHIEU	(6)
NOUVION-EN-PONTHIEU	23rd	1.45 pm	arrived NOUVION-EN-PONTHIEU	

WAR DIARY or INTELLIGENCE SUMMARY

Army Form C. 2118.

Place	Date	Hour	Summary of Events and Information	Remarks and references to Appendices
NOUVION EN PONTHIEU	Nov 24th		Joining. The following joined from Base for duty S/399196 J. DINGWALL. S/3970 Pte J.A. BRITTON. 940670 # DICHBURN. S/384706. T.H. HOWARTH.	
Do.	24th 11am		Pte L. SHIPSTONE departed from here in England.	(Y)
ARRY	24th 1.45pm		Left for ARRY - ambulance. Main finished at 1.45 pm.	
ARRY	25th		Arrived ARRY, proceeded to arrange place for Hospital. Cleaned up billets. Hospital accommodation very limited - number = 18.	
ARRY	26th		Parade at 10 am mending & cleaning equipment. List of deficiencies in kit, equipment, medical stores, Rainproof to be made out & handed into Orderly Room. Orderly & Tent Sub Division take over duty in hospital. Precautions against fire in Billets - Notices made out & hung up in each billet.	
Do.	27		Necessary fatigues. Clean - S/3077 Sergt C BROOKE S/3307 Pte J. DAWSON S/3322 Pte J DARCH #18.4 L S/3948 Pte COWEY To England. Rodrig Captain Infirmary and Capt Hamilton came forth to B Field Ambulance Company, signed from hours 6.3 "Pu Ord")	
Do.	28th		Attached - Capt Eagles, accorded for temp duty with 144 Howitzer Bty	

2353 Wt. W2544/1454 700,000 5/15 D.D.&L. A.D.S.S./Forms/C. 2118.

Army Form C. 2118.

WAR DIARY
or
INTELLIGENCE SUMMARY.
(Erase heading not required.)

Place	Date	Hour	Summary of Events and Information	Remarks and references to Appendices
#RRY.	Nov 29th		Route march — troops not on special fatigues. Staff & 3 van Corpl Trans in charge. Medical order — Parade daily at 9-15 a.m. (except for Div Trains) orderly Officer to take Parade in absence of O.C. Officer of Sub. Div? Except M.O. on duty in Hospital Latrine.	
ARRY.	30th		Route march at 9-15 a.m. Surgeon Adam in charge. Necessary fatigues. Routine —	

A.F. Fleming
Staff Surgeon RN
O.C. 1st Field Ambulance
63rd (RN) Div.

MESSAGES AND SIGNALS. — Army Form C. 2121

TO: No 1 Field Ambulance

Sender's Number: GW 171
Day of Month: 17
AAA

No 1 Field Ambulance will march at noon vice ACHEUX, LEALVILLERS, ARQUEVES, RAINCHEVAL, Cross roads three quarters mile north-west of RAINCHEVAL, thence by northern end of BEAUQUESNES to northern end of BEAUVAL where they will join 188th Inf Brigade group AAA Billeting parties will be sent ahead to BEAUVAL to report to Town major AAA Addressed No 1 Field Ambulance, repeated 188th Inf Brigade and Fifth Corps. AAA Acknowledge

From: 63 Div
Place:
Time: 8.36 am

"A" Form
MESSAGES AND SIGNALS.   Army Form C. 2121

No. of Message ....

Prefix .... Code .... m. | Words | Charge | This message is on a/c of: | Recd. at .... m.
Office of Origin and Service Instructions | Sent | | .... Service. | Date
Copy | At .... m. | | | From
| To | | (Signature of "Franking Officer.") | By
| By | | |

TO No 1 Field Ambulance

Sender's Number | Day of Month | In reply to Number | AAA
* BM 780 | 18/11/16 | |

You will be ready to move tomorrow at 9-30 am aaa

From 188 Inf Brigade
Place
Time

Copy.

"A" Form
MESSAGES AND SIGNALS.

Army Form C. 2121

Date (3)

TO O.C. No 1 Field Ambulance.

Sender's Number: BM 804
Day of Month: 29/11/16

AAA

You will be prepared to move at 9.30 AM tomorrow. Length of march 6 miles.

From 188 Inf Brigade
Time 2.30pm

Copy

"A" Form
MESSAGES AND SIGNALS.

Army Form C. 2121

To 188th Inf Brigade Order No 60

Day of Month: 20-11-16

AAA

1. The Brigade will move tomorrow to the CRAMONT - COULONVILLERS area.

2. 1st Field Ambulance will move to YVRENCH.

"A" Form
MESSAGES AND SIGNALS.

Army Form C. 2121

TO | 188 Inf. Brigade Order No. 61.

Day of Month: 21-11-16

AAA

I. The Brigade will move tomorrow to the BRAILLY area

II. 1st Field Ambulance will move to FONTAINE-SUR-MAYE.

Copy

"A" Form
MESSAGES AND SIGNALS.

Army Form C. 2121

| To | 188th Inf Brigade Order No 62 |

Day of Month
22-11-16

AAA

I The Brigade will move tomorrow to LE TITRE area. aaa

II The 1st Field Ambce will move to NOUVION-EN-PONTHIEU aaa

"A" Form
MESSAGES AND SIGNALS.

Army Form C. 2121

TO: 188th Inf Brigade Order No 63

Day of Month: 23-11-16.

AAA

I. The Brigade will move tomorrow

II. The 1st Field Amb^{ce} will move to ARRY. aaa

MEDICAL

CONFIDENTIAL.

VOLUME 7.

WAR DIARY

of

1ST FIELD AMBULANCE 63 (R.N.) DIVN.

FROM 1ST DECEMBER 1916

TO 31ST DECEMBER 1916

STAFF SURGEON, R.N.
O.C. 1ST FIELD AMBCE. R.N.D.

Army Form C. 2118.

WAR DIARY
or
INTELLIGENCE SUMMARY.
(Erase heading not required.)

Instructions regarding War Diaries and Intelligence Summaries are contained in F. S. Regs., Part II. and the Staff Manual respectively. Title pages will be prepared in manuscript.

Place	Date	Hour	Summary of Events and Information	Remarks and references to Appendices
ARRY	1916. Dec. 1st		Route March from 9.15 to 11.45 a.m.	
	2nd		Incinery Fatigues. Posting – S/3265 Pte W. BALMFORTH to A Tent. S/3265 Pte G. OATES to A Tent. S/3994 Pte J. GREEN to A Tent. S/3110 Pte R. LEE to C Beurex. S/3997 Pte H. DINGWELL to C Beurex. S/4067 Pte A. DITCHBURN to E Beurex. S/3990 Pte J. A. BRITTON to B Beurex. S/3847 Pte TH. HOWARTH to B Beurex.	
"	3rd		Inspection Parade 10 a.m. Transport Inspection 11 a.m. Inspection Billets 10.30.	
"	4th	9.30 am	Duty A Tent Sub. Division. Take over Hospital duties from C Tent. Route March. Capt TIMMS in Charge. 10 Tent Sub-division & R.D. held for duty with 44. C.C.S returned for duty. Men + Precautions against fire in Billets read out on Parade.	
"	5th	9.30	Guard drill – 9.30. Leave to England – Following proceeded on leave last evening:– S/3279 Sto/Sergt S. WALSH. S/3246 Pte J. NELSON. S/3644 ... S/3372 Pte A.E. COOPER. S/3344 Pte J HASWELL	

WAR DIARY
or
INTELLIGENCE SUMMARY.
(Erase heading not required.)

Army Form C. 2118.

Place	Date	Hour	Summary of Events and Information	Remarks and references to Appendices
ARRY.	Dec 6th	9.15	Squad Drill – 9.15. Lecture on 1st Aid – 10.30 to 11.30 am. Nursing Lectures.	
DO	7th		Route March – 9.15 to 11.45 am. 1.30 pm to 2.30 Lecture on Nursing duties – 2.30 pm to 4 pm Football	
DO	8th		Route March – 9.15 am to 11.45 am. Afternoon – 9/3786 Pte H. CRUSWELL appointed Temp Provisional Lance Corpl (unpaid) while in charge of Sanitary Party	
DO	9th		Tent duty – Capt Matthews Revue to 2 R.M. Battⁿ. Squad drill – 9-30 am to 10-30 am. Afternoon – Same Inspection Parade – 10 am Inspection Billets 10-30 Inspection Transport – 11 am	
DO	10th		Duty. B. Zull take over Hospt duties from A. Zull. The following O.R. report to O.C Sunday for course of Instruction 9/3761 PG J.T. LIVESAY 9/3531 Pte E. HENDERSON 9/3072 Cpl. F. KEATING, Relief Capt Boyle & Batman returned from Temp duty with 14th WORCES Bayⁿ.	
DO	11th		Route March – 9.30 to 11-30 am. 1-30 pm Lecture – Sanitation	

Army Form C. 2118.

WAR DIARY
or
INTELLIGENCE SUMMARY.
(Erase heading not required.)

Instructions regarding War Diaries and Intelligence Summaries are contained in F. S. Regs., Part II. and the Staff Manual respectively. Title pages will be prepared in manuscript.

Place	Date	Hour	Summary of Events and Information	Remarks and references to Appendices
ARRY	Dec 12th	11-30 am	**MOVE** 1st Field Ambulance with Stores & Transport moved from ARRY to VRON	See Appendix 1.
VRON	12th	12:50	Ambulance arrived at VRON and proceeded to establish a Hospital. Men went into billets. The following left for England on leave to England:— S/3129 Sergt J.A. SWAIN. S/3371 Cpl. J. MARTIN. S/3232 Pte. E.H. GREENWOOD. S/2451 Pte. S. BATT (Orig. Train).	
VRON	13th		**Fatigues** Opening up Hospital. 7B with Erection of NISSEN HUT. Making Cookhouse, Latrines & Washhouses & Latrines.	
VRON	14th		Orderly: Lieut. J.P. BROWN came to work in Batt (Authority Comm. 63rd Fd Amb m). The following DR 1st Field Ambces awarded the Military Medal:— S/3304 L/Cpl Sergt N. ELLIOTT. S/3232 Pte. E.H. GREENWOOD. S/3894 Pte W. THORP. Orderly Lieut J.H. Clement joined 1st Field Ambce from 14th Wessex Batt for duty. Fatigues Preparing Hospital.	

Place	Date	Hour	Summary of Events and Information	Remarks and references to Appendices
VRON.	Dec. 15th		Medical Orders - All recent instructions issued in orders in regards precautions against lice in billets are to be strictly enforced.	
		1-1.15pm	Coy. Parade.	
			Orderly. The following temperaments from Base joined yesterday. S/3968 Pte G. McCourt, S/3801 Pte E. Mills S/4164 Pte A. Morris S/4181 Pte E. Wilson G/4134 Pte S.R. Yearsley.	
			Return to Hospital -	
			Leave to England. The following left for England on leave - S/3406 Sergt Rees, S/3276 Sergt Tumberlain, S/3203 Corpl Smith, S/3121 Pte Wreq S/3224 Pte G. Yeoman, S/3065 Pte E. Mutchamp, S/3273 Pte S. Harper, S/3331 Pte T. Oliver, S/3410 Pte T. Bell, S/3414 Pte J. Vickers, S/1705 Z/4144 Bruinster (for 7 days) S/1852 Pte Barker (for 7 am)	
VRON.	16th		Staff Surgeon A.I. Fleming to England on leave. Temp. Surgeon Kay mobilised act on Lt. 1st Field Amble. during its absence on leave of Staff Surgn Fleming. Orderly. Lieut. E.H. Clements to C. Tuet.	

WAR DIARY or INTELLIGENCE SUMMARY

Army Form C. 2118.

Place	Date	Hour	Summary of Events and Information	Remarks and references to Appendices
VRON	Feb 16th		Temp duty - Capt V Eagles Rouse to 1st Res Batt for lunch duty	
VRON	17th		272531 Pte G.W. McDONALD (Br. Train) att 1st FA admitted Temp. Provisional Sauce Corpl (returned)	
VRON	18th	10 am	MOVE 1st Field Ambulance with Stores & Advanced Moved at 10am to April 2 from VRON to NEMPONT ST FIRMIN	
NEMPONT	18th	11 am	Ambulance arrived at NEMPONT-ST-FIRMIN & proceeded to establish a Hospl. Men prepared billets only 6 tents took over reproductn from R tent	
"	19th		Fatigues cleaning up Horse lines & grounds, making latrines incinerator, woodhouse, cookhouse, Breakfasthouse Hut	
"	20th		Fatigues on Hops & billets. 2pm delivered on Sanitation Route march 9.30 am. An officer and others daily at ARRY to see dead shirked men. D.S. G. 158th M.C. Coy + 188th French Huntini by Lorry Ambulance at 9 am in Ambulance Car & calling at VERCOURT and VILLERS-sous-AUTTHIE for Reducen proving probably by Henry & Aubery Bois.	

and VILLERS-sous-AUTTHIE

Army Form C. 2118.

WAR DIARY
or
INTELLIGENCE SUMMARY.
(Erase heading not required.)

Place	Date	Hour	Summary of Events and Information	Remarks and references to Appendices
NEMPONT	Dec 21st		Fatigues. On Hospital & Billets. Route march at 9.30 am	
NEMPONT	22nd		Joining The following T.R.'s joined yesterday from Base. S/4145 Pte H Dunday S/3471 Pte D Jenkin S/4017 Pte W.W. Robson. S/3798 Pte G Lindsay S/3970 Pte J Singleton. Route march at 9.30 am. Instruction in water carts. Bombing. Lecture at 10 am. Inoculation against Typhoid & Paratyphoid at 2 pm.	
NEMPONT	23rd		Fatigues on Hospital & Billets. Leave to England. The following Officers & O.R. left for England today. Surgeon J.R. Adam. S/3057 Sergt R Ward S/3186 Corpl W Hill. S/3199 Sergt. C Surgeon S/3808 Pte J.S. Bennett. S/3370 Pte G.W. Payne S/3313 Pte S. Nelson S/3357 Pte A Lord S/3383 W Holmes S/1771 L/Cpl T.H. Nelson S/1600 Pte R H West. S/3870 Pte T Dawes Bombing Lecture on burying bodies at 11 am. Masonry fatigues	

WAR DIARY
or
INTELLIGENCE SUMMARY.

Place	Date	Hour	Summary of Events and Information	Remarks and references to Appendices
NIEUPORT	Dec 24th	10 am	Inspection Parade at 10 am. Inspection of Transport 11 am. Inspected buses & tents. Take our usual duties from C Tent.	
Do	25th		Greetings from HQ & officers to NCO's Men. Service in Sanctuary at 1-30 pm by Sergt. Hay. Money. Received from above Lieu t. Sergt. Major Barrow. Sergt. Sergt. N. Elliot will act as acting Sergeant Major. Honorary Patrons.	
Do	26th		Snow fell 9.15 & 10-15 am. Leaving on & preceding to be taken a Samfit of a Gas attack by Germans at 10-15. Lecture on "Controlli of Gunners" at 11 am by Capt. Matthew Reeve. Returned and from same.	
Do	27th		Sergt. Sivain, Cpl. Martin, & Cpl. Greenwood on Patrol. Promotions. The following promotions made to date from 16th Dec. S/266.S Cpl. S. Barlow to Sergeant Clerk S/3186 L/Cpl. W. Hill to Corporal S/3036. Acv. Cpl. J. Holmes to Corpl. S/3831 Pte W. Titley to Lance Corpl. S/ Pte E. H. Drewmont to Lance Corpl. S/ 3971 Pte. N. Sellers to Lance Corpl.	
Do	28th			

WAR DIARY
or
INTELLIGENCE SUMMARY.
(Erase heading not required.)

Army Form C. 2118.

Place	Date	Hour	Summary of Events and Information	Remarks and references to Appendices
NIEMPONT & St. FIRMIN	28th		Routine. Church Parade 9.30 a.m. Lecture on Cleaning of Instruments at 1-30 p.m. — Surg. Major Matheson Necessary fatigues.	
Do.	29th		Routine 9.15 to 10 a.m. Physical Drill 10 a.m. Lecture on Medical Stores Order. Given by Lt Clements Recue to D.A.C. 63rd Div in lieu of Capt Lawrence Rawe who will join 1st Field Ambce Anthony's Ptens 63rd Div "	
Do.	30th		Physical Drill - Stafflergts Strutt, Brewer, Sergt Jaulechun Leavg. Reed See Corpl Brewer, Cpl Smith Pte Haynes to a Germany. Pte Barker. Going from leave - Pte Mullerdorg, Pte Oliver Pte Vickers Pte Hunt, Pte Bell. S.	
Do.	31st		The following proceeded on leave to England yesterday - Surg. Maj. Thomas, Sergt Meeson, Corpl Jelly, Pte Yates, Pte Bulley Pte Paine, Pte Ruffett, Pte Capps (who on Tram attached. Inspection 9. on 63rd " inspected ambulance & expressed him as pleased with arrangements Made. A. J. Henry Lt Col. 63rd M.R.C. Div " Necessary fatigues.	

"A" Form.
MESSAGES AND SIGNALS.

Army Form C.2121
(in pads of 100).
No. of Message ....

TO 1st Field Ambulance
63 (RN) Divn

Sender's Number: Brigade Order No 68
Day of Month: 11-12-16

AAA

1st Field Ambulance will move to VRON tomorrow the 12th inst. Time for passing starting point 11-30 am AAA

From 188 Brigade Hd Qrs.

"A" Form.
MESSAGES AND SIGNALS.

Army Form C.2121
(in pads of 100).

TO: 1st Field Ambulance

Sender's Number.	Day of Month.	In reply to Number.	
* BM 938	16.12.16		AAA

1st Field Ambulance will move to NEMPONT-ST-FIRMIN on the 18th inst. AAA. Time for passing starting point 10 am. AAA.

From 188 B.H.Q.

MEDICAL.

CONFIDENTIAL.

VOLUME 9.

WAR DIARY

of

1st FIELD AMBULANCE

63rd (RN) DIVISION

FROM.   13th JANUARY 1917

To   31st JANUARY 1917

A.C.R. Lutton
Captain RAMC.
O.C. 1st Field Amb.
63 (R.N.) Divn

WAR DIARY
INTELLIGENCE SUMMARY

Army Form C. 2118.

Place	Date	Hour	Summary of Events and Information	Remarks and references to Appendices
NEMPONT St. FIRMIN	1917 Jan 1st	Morning	Capt. LAVERICK Rame Joined from E Tent Sub-division	
		July	B Tent Sub-division taken over Hospital duties from A Tent at 9 a.m. Working parties - on hospital outbuildings, wash & bath houses to be four up. whitewashing buildings.	
Do	2nd	Morning	Capt. Boyden & Batman from 1 MR.M. Bn't Course of Cookery - S/40010 Pt J WILMAN to join Cookery School of Instruction at RUE.	
			Routine - Parade 9.15 - Lecture on Nursing duties - on M.Beav 1.0 - at 5 a.m. Squad drill - 9.30 - to 10-30 a.m. Pony parade - 1-30 p.m	
Do	3rd	Morning	Following to complete link o Bearer - Subdivision. Sergt Barlow to B Tent Corpl Crush, Corpl W Hill to C Bearer Corpl J Holmes to A Bearer Corpl S A Bolt to B Bearer, Lee Cpl W Tetley to B Bearer, Lee Cpl Sutton to B Tent Lee Cpl J A Greenwood to C Bearer Lee Cpl R McKenzie to B Tent Pte T Brown to B Tent the following to A Bearer Ptes C Tordmanen W Doughty, W Green, C L Handsman J Walsh H Sage W S Jones	

1st FIELD AMBULANCE,
63rd (R.N.) DIVISION

WAR DIARY or INTELLIGENCE SUMMARY

Army Form C. 2118.

Place	Date	Hour	Summary of Events and Information	Remarks and references to Appendices
NEMPONT ST FIRMIN	1917 Jan 3rd		The following W.B. Reivers – Ptes. A Wilson, J Wilkinson, W.A. Wild, L Hempenny, T Wilson, J Armstrong, W Behan, E Clarke, J H Walmsley & Mills. The following to E Beevers Ptes E Marshall, H Bradley & Murray, W N Robson, J Livvy, J Hurbottle, H Lees, W Lees, J Bingham, F Bradley, S.R Yearsley, D Jenkins, H Baxendale. Supernumerii Pte B. Green to A Tent. Pte J McCourt to B Tent. Pte J Wrighton to C Beevers. Pte J Cammish to E Beevers. Pte T Scrafton to B Beevers. For Half day course at Div "San School" – the following officers – N.C.Os to attend for ½ day course at Div "San School" at R.U.E. Capt Matthews. Revr. Capt Truman Rawe. Sergt Townsley. Corpl Bott. 2/Cpl Back. J Greenwood. Routine Parade at 9.15 am Sewers cleared at 9.30. Lecture on Medical Carriers at 11 am. Games & Football at 1.20 p.m. Tenth duty. Capt LAVERICK Raine W1/N.F.C. for Kings duty. Routine – Route March 9.30 to 11-45 am. Parade without Box Resp – 1-30 pm	

1st FIELD AMBULANCE. 63RD (R.N.) DIVISION.

Army Form C. 2118.

WAR DIARY
or
INTELLIGENCE SUMMARY.
(Erase heading not required.)

Instructions regarding War Diaries and Intelligence Summaries are contained in F. S. Regs., Part II. and the Staff Manual respectively. Title pages will be prepared in manuscript.

Place	Date	Hour	Summary of Events and Information	Remarks and references to Appendices
NEWPONT St FIRMIN	Jan 5th		Routine Parade - 9-15. Physical Drill - 9.30 to 10 am. Stretcher Ambulance Staves 10 am to 11-30 am. Lecture on "Use + care of Instruments" 1.30 to 2.30 pm. Stretcher Staves 2.30 hrs to R.	
do	6th		Posting. Pte H. Crispin S/3747 and Pte A. Hamilton S/4163 to R. Review on Superannuation. Leave to England. The following left for England on leave - Sergt Holmes, Sergt Ferguson, L/Cpl Gummerson, Pte Beck, in hospital, Pte Reece, Pte Saunders, Pte Clapper, Pte Ogden, Pte Payne (via Trans Act). Medical order Officers of Sub. Divisions to cause all trenches used as urinals to be closed, and that all PCO's urinals are for to present to the Frinie Shortly, O.H.G. helmets to be returned to BM Stores. Routine Squad drill 9.30 to 10-30. Lecture on tuberculosis 10.45 to 11-45. Training Parties on Horse trucking. Board of survey to submit a concession for a Repair commission of Indian Army Stretcher in Orderly Room 10-30 today. President: Capt Matthews. Members: Capt Saylen + Capt Jennings.	

FIELD AMBULANCE, 63rd (R.N.) DIVISION.

Army Form C. 2118.

WAR DIARY
or
INTELLIGENCE SUMMARY.
(Erase heading not required.)

Instructions regarding War Diaries and Intelligence Summaries are contained in F.S. Regs., Part II. and the Staff Manual respectively. Title pages will be prepared in manuscript.

Place	Date	Hour	Summary of Events and Information	Remarks and references to Appendices
NEWPONT BAINS FIRMIN	Jan 7th		Routine Inspection parade – 10 am. Inspection billets 10-30 am Inspection transport 11 am.	
DO.	8th		Duty. 2 Inns Sub division will take over Hospt duties from B Sub division. Joining T/15731 Staff/Sergt Major C. E. HARMAN. a/c W. O (1st Cl.) Joined Ambulance for duty from No 2 Coy Dis Train Re-joining Ptes J.T. Livesey, H.T Butterworth, Fallen, T. Keating M.Wilkinson rejoined from course of Stretcher work Repair log Route march 9.30 parade 9-15 am . lecture on "Precautions against Gas attack"	
Routine			Route march - 9.30 to 11. 45. Parade. 9.15 am. Routemarch "Gas Helmet Drill" If weather does not permit a Route march "Precautions against Gas attack" 9.30 - to 10-30. lecture on Sanitation 1-30 - to 2-30 pm (Capt Boyle, J. (Surg Adam)	
DO.	9th		Fire Precaut. For present Off of 20 men to be always told off & ready Billets to be marked "Fire Picquet".	

1ST FIELD AMBULANCE.
63RD (R.N.) DIVISION.

WAR DIARY
or
INTELLIGENCE SUMMARY.

Army Form C. 2118.

Place	Date	Hour	Summary of Events and Information	Remarks and references to Appendices
NEMPONT ST FIRMIN	Jan 10th		Leave all men proceeding on leave must either train kits, Knives forks & spoons. Transport inspected by Corps Commander. Routine Parade 9-15 am. Company drill 9-30 - 10-30 am. Lecture on trench Regimen 11 am to 11-45 am. 1-30 pm Football & Games.	
Do	11th		Rotation duty. Capt Mathews Ramie attached for sanity duty with 14th Worcestin Batt. Left at 7-15 am Cablery to Jones Batt. Move. Field Ambulance to St. Remay to Cause present billets in 13th will Surplus Stores & billet Stores Sent to Div Dump at Rue (Rue des Fours). Latrine buckets returned. Temp. Latrine dug which will be filled in & numbered before leaving on 13th will. Disposal of Patients. All Seating & Patients likely to be fit for duty in a few days transferred to 2nd field ambulance, LE CROTOY, others to be	

[Stamp: 1st FIELD AMBULANCE RAMC (R.N.) DIVISION]

Army Form C. 2118.

WAR DIARY
or
INTELLIGENCE SUMMARY.
(Erase heading not required.)

Instructions regarding War Diaries and Intelligence Summaries are contained in F. S. Regs., Part II. and the Staff Manual respectively. Title pages will be prepared in manuscript.

FIELD AMBULANCE.
1ST
63RD (R.N.) DIVISION.
No.................
Date..............

Place	Date	Hour	Summary of Events and Information	Remarks and references to Appendices
NEMPONT St. FIRMIN	Jan. 11th		Succeeded by 9th Canadian Gen. Hospital. ETAPLES!	
			Routine Parade 9.15 a.m. Physical Drill 9.30 to 11.45 a.m. Gas Helmet Drill 1.30 pm to 2.30 pm. Necessary working parties.	
Do.	12th		Mobilization Stores - packed on transport wagons.	
			Move Parade at 8 a.m. transport wagons. Leave at 8.15 a.m. for NOUVION. Billeting Party (Surgn. ADAM) will leave at 9.30 a.m. tomorrow.	
Do.	13th		Medical wear - Officers of Sub Divisions to inspect Mens' wear by their Detachments weekly. See that - Iron Rations, Gas Helmets Box Respirators, Goggles are correct & seen in proper Sts.	
			Weekly Return by 12 noon Saturday each week.	
			Motor Ambulance & steam from Ept. NEMPONT St. FIRMIN at 8.15 a.m.	
			COMMAND. Capt. R.T.C. ROBERTSON assumed Command of 1st Field Ambulance from today 13.1.17. (Authority, DMS s/wing NoP. 3/57 dated 10.1.17).	

A.Y. Fleming
Staff Surgn RN

Army Form C. 2118.

WAR DIARY
or
INTELLIGENCE SUMMARY.
(Erase heading not required.)

Instructions regarding War Diaries and Intelligence Summaries are contained in F.S. Regs., Part II. and the Staff Manual respectively. Title pages will be prepared in manuscript.

Place	Date	Hour	Summary of Events and Information	Remarks and references to Appendices
NEMPONT ST FIRMIN	13-1-17	2pm	Ambulance and Transport arrived NOUVION 2pm	PCR
NOUVION	14-1-17		Ambulance left NOUVION 9.15 a.m with transport and proceeded to FROYELLES arriving 12 noon.	PCR
FROYELLES	15-1-17		Ambulance with transport left FROYELLES at 8-30 a.m and proceeded to LE MEILLARD arriving 5-30 p.m.	PCR
LE MEILLARD	16-1-17	10 A.M.	Ambulance at rest. Staff Surg. A.P. Fleming (RN), Surg J R Kay-Mouat (RN), Surg J R Adam (RN) reported to Admiralty (Anthony) ADMS 109/53. D. 16/1/17. The following Officers joined the Ambulance for duty, Capt J. McGREGOR RAMC. Capt M.A. POWER RAMC; Capt E.C.D. PELLIER RAMC.; Lieut J. YOUNG RAMC. auth. ADMS. 72/202 D. 16/1/17	PCR
LE MEILLARD	17-1-17	11 A.M.	Advance party left 8-30 a.m. for main Dressing Station, LANCASHIRE DUMP. Stores over from 35 F.P. AMB. Advance party consisted of Capt. T. MMS. RAMC, Capt. POWER RAMC. Lieut and Qr Mr WILLIAMS, two N.C.O.'s and Six Privates RAMC. Ambulance left 9-15 a.m with transport and proceeded to BEAUQUESNES.	PCR
BEAUQUESNES	19/1/17		Ambulance arrived with transport 5-5 pm. Capt LAVERICK RAMC.T. rejoined Field Ambulance at Head Qrs 7pm having been attached on Temporary duty with 12th H.A.G	PCR

WAR DIARY
or
INTELLIGENCE SUMMARY
(Erase heading not required.)

Army Form C. 2118.

Place	Date	Hour	Summary of Events and Information	Remarks and references to Appendices
BEAUQUESNE	18/1/17		Field Ambulance and Transport left at 8.45 am and proceeded BLANGERMIE DUMP at CLAIRFAYE. Transport was detached and left with transport of No 3 Field Amb. under charge of O.C. No 3 F.Amb. The move was completed at 5 p.m. Reliefs for Advanced Dressing Station and Relay posts took over at 3.30 pm from 36. F. Amb.; Capt. Power took over Advanced Dressing Station at St PIERRE DIVION, Capt Timms passed to A.D.S. THIEPVAL.	MCR
LANCASHIRE DUMP	19/1/17	10 AM	Inspected the Camp and found that accommodation reserved for WS sitting cases in Dug outs Field was one uncompleted hut. There is no accommodation from the Sanitorial Point of view and room was inadequate. Portable stove undesirable. Position from time and Latrines too close to Hospital.	MCR
" "	20/1/17		The following Officers were posted to Subdivisions. Capt. LAVERICK to A. Tent. Capt. POWER Ramc to B. Bearers, Capt PEILER to B. Tent. Capt McGREGOR and Lieut YOUNG to C. Tent. I visited, alongwith Capt EAGLES, the Advanced Dressing station at THIEPVAL and went over the ground in front with Capt TIMMS and made arrangements about the mountain tramwail.	MCR
" "	21-1-17		The following N.C.O.s and men are granted leave to ENGLAND from 21-1-17 to 31-1-17. Cpl HOLMES, L/Cpl TITLEY, Pte WEEDY, Pte TITLEY, Pte LIVSEY, Pte WAITES, Pte NUNN Pte BEBRICK, Pte STENLAKE Pte BAIN. Visited St Pierre Divion Advanced Dressing station and found that equipment that sufficient and personnel comfortable. The following Ord. photo for club from leave to England: Sgt Ferguson, L/Cpl Emmerson	MCR

WAR DIARY or INTELLIGENCE SUMMARY

Army Form C. 2118.

Place	Date	Hour	Summary of Events and Information	Remarks and references to Appendices
Rame Dump	24/1/17		Pte Saunders, Pte Chapman, Pte Moffatt, A Bywater, Pte Paare, Pte Rich, Pte Bain.	arh
"	2/1/17	noon	Extensive silt clearance and accommodation enlarged; new stores constructed for horses on other side of road and away from the hospital. One hut for such and wounded men completed. The work of erecting other huts and road constructions continued. A D.M.S of Division and D.D.M.S of Corps visited the field ambulance.	arh
"	25/1/17	noon	Work of building accommodation for sick and wounded in progress.	arh
"	26/1/17	6 pm	Capt Eagles along with D.D.M.S visited the A.D.S TINEPARK and Regimental Aid Posts in BULGAR Trench and expects an alternative road for evacuation of wounded in the event of active operations. Something special to report. O.C. troops made visit the building which	arh
"	25/1/17	5 pm	A.D.M.S of the Division. D.D.M.S of Corps made reconnaissance and proceeded to the A.D. station at St. PIERRE. DIVION. Transport Capt EAGLES. RAMC opposite Sanitary officer for the 188 Infantry Brigade area.	arh
"	27/1/17	6 pm	attended a conference at A.D.M.S Offices.	arh
"	29/1/17	9 pm	Capt TIMMS, R.A.M.C. took over change from Lt Young, R.A.M.C the advanced Dressing station at St PIERRE. DIVION. Lt YOUNG returned to Head Quarters of the Ambulance.	arh

WAR DIARY
or
INTELLIGENCE SUMMARY.

Army Form C. 2118.

Place	Date	Hour	Summary of Events and Information	Remarks and references to Appendices
LANCASHIRE DUMP	29/1/17	6pm	Received Copy No.1 of Preliminary Operation Orders No.14 ADMS. One Motor Hospital Frozen hut Completed. For the recreation evacuation of MDS casualty cases. Since that has made the Motor Transport almost immovable. Received a report from O.C. No. H.T. Co. (Motor) that sliding doors cars cannot run by Rivers input for the work up. This continues the present condition.	acR
"	30/1/17	6pm	Considerable progress made with the building of hospital accommodation. The Aluminium and Point "Rivers Posts" and Armoured Advanced Dressing Stations have been fully & equipped in accordance with A.D.M.S. orders noted 24/1/17. No 17/1/44.	acR
"	31/1/17	6pm	A.D.M.S. visits Field Ambulance. Critical complete and there is now accommodation for three hundred sick and wounded.	acR

P.C.F. Tinsdale
Captain RAMC.
O.C. No. F.A. Ambce
63 (RN) D.

MEDICAL

CONFIDENTIAL.

VOLUME

WAR DIARY

OF

1ST FIELD AMBULANCE

63RD (R.N.) DIVN

FROM 1ST FEBRUARY 1917

TO 28TH FEBRUARY 1917.

A.S.E. Rhutherford
Lieut. Colonel R.A.M.C.
O.C. 1st Fd Ambce
63 (R.N.) Divn.

WAR DIARY
or
INTELLIGENCE SUMMARY.

Army Form C. 2118.

Place	Date	Hour	Summary of Events and Information	Remarks and references to Appendices
Lancashire Dump	1/2/17	6pm	Capt Timms Rame proceeded to A.D.S St Pierre Divion. Lt Young reported head - Orderlies & ambulance. Received ammunition and rations by permission order A.D.M.S N° 19.	nil
	2/2/17	6pm	Nothing special to report.	nil
	3/2/17	6pm	All arrangements complete according to F.D.M.S order N° 15. by 12 noon. 11pm unusual activity not artillery on support.	nil
	4/2/17	6pm	12.15 am the wounded cases arrived. 2 am infantry lines bombarded, working parties arrived. Brigade arranging stretcher and walking wounded. 1 at Mountaineros Station 4 walkers and walking wounded. 3 via Kentish. By midnight 15 officers and 173 other ranks passed through the ambulance. 3 other Ranks died. Prisoners 1 her wounded 1 officer and 11 other Ranks. D.D.M.S & others visits the Ambulance at 3.0 pm.	nil
	5/2/17	6pm	Wounded continue to arrive in large numbers. The staff and personnel at main Dressing Station are working at high pressure to cope with the situation. By midnight 8 officers and 226 other ranks were cleared and fed and evacuated to C.C.S. Five German prisoners of war were also dealt with. Impossible to hut nearing completion. A few of the wounded arrived with frozen hands and feet.	nil

WAR DIARY or INTELLIGENCE SUMMARY

Army Form C. 2118.

Place	Date	Hour	Summary of Events and Information	Remarks and references to Appendices
Lancashire Dump	6/2/17	6pm	Casualties admitted to Main Dressing Station. Officers Nil. O.R. 32. Prisoners of war 2.	PMM
"	7/2/17	6pm	Casualties admitted to M.D.S. Officers 2. O.R. 9. The Commander II Corps visited the Ambulance this afternoon on completion of operations. He asked that the officers of the Ambulance be assembled and expressed himself as highly satisfied with the work done by them and congratulated them — Operation Order No 20. A.D.M.S. received.	ack
"	8/2/17	6pm	Casualties admitted to M.D.S. Officers 1. Other ranks 86. German Prisoners Officers 2 — Other ranks 6. The Divisional Commander Major General SHUTE visited this Ambulance this morning and complimented the Ambulance on the good work they had done during the recent operations. Made a reconnaissance of the ground between St Pierre Divion and Grant[court] with the view of selecting a forward site for an A.D.S. and found a suitable site in O.G.I. Map ref Sheet 57D France - R9d 2.2. Received Operation Order No 21.	AMM R9d 2.2

Army Form C. 2118.

WAR DIARY
or
INTELLIGENCE SUMMARY.
(Erase heading not required.)

Place	Date	Hour	Summary of Events and Information	Remarks and references to Appendices
LANCASHIRE DUMP.	9/2/17	6 p.m	Casualties. Officers 3 Other Ranks 36. German prisoners 2. German prisoners handed over to 56th Field Ambulance. The A.D.S. at ST PIERRE DIVION.	nil
"	10/2/17	6 p.m.	Casualties - Officers nil Other Ranks 2.	nil
"	11/2/17	6 p.m	Casualties. Officers nil Other Ranks 5. Received Home Operation Order No. 22 - Map Ref Sheet 57ᴰSE. The Sanitary Officer of 5th Army visited the main dressing Station -	nil
"	12/2/17	6 p.m.	Casualties. Officers nil Other Ranks 7. Capt Irwin R.A.M.C. proceeded with 2 N.C.O's and 4 men to acquaint himself with the positions of and routes of evacuation from the R.A.P's of Assaulting Battalions.	nil

Army Form C. 2118.

WAR DIARY
or
INTELLIGENCE SUMMARY.
(Erase heading not required.)

Instructions regarding War Diaries and Intelligence Summaries are contained in F. S. Regs., Part II. and the Staff Manual respectively. Title pages will be prepared in manuscript.

Place	Date	Hour	Summary of Events and Information	Remarks and references to Appendices
LANCASHIRE DUMP	13/2/17	6pm	Casualties Officers Nil. Other Ranks 1. Capt Timms & Capt Pellier R.A.M.C. proceeded to Aveley Post taking with them 2 N.C.O's and to the 54th Field Ambulance, and 8 other ranks in two motor ambulances, to make themselves acquainted with the routes of evacuation worked by the Field Ambulance. Sanitary Officer 21st San Section visited Capt Campwell Young this Ambulance.	AKB
" "	14/2/17	6pm	Casualties Officers 2. Other Ranks 15.	AKB
" "	15/2/17	6pm	Casualties Officers Nil Other Ranks 10. Received A.D.M.S Operation Orders No 23. No S/4144 Pte CLARK proceeded to A.D.M.S Office and was struck off W. Strength. No S/3058 Bgr HOLMES R. No S/3610 Pte DEBRICK W. S/3642 Pte A STENLAKE. No S/4145 Pte DUDLEY H.E. Proceeded to No 1 Territorial Base Depot Rouen No S/4145 Pte DAVIS H. S/3670 Proceeded to England and were struck off the Strength Pte DAVIS being a candidate for Temporary Infantry Commission and was struck off the Strength.	AKB

A.5834 Wt. W4973/M687 D750,000 8/16 D. D. & L. Ltd. Forms/C.2118/13

WAR DIARY or INTELLIGENCE SUMMARY

Army Form C. 2118.

Place	Date	Hour	Summary of Events and Information	Remarks and references to Appendices
LANCASHIRE DUMP	16/2/17	6 p.m	Casualties Officers Nil. OR.13. Received 188th Bde Operation Orders No 82. No82/1, No82/2, No62/3, No82/4 Received Bonus No M×S 1/17 dated 14/2/17 and 5th Army D.M.S. No 16/337 dated 14/2/17. Promotions S/8205 Cpl TILLEY R.S. to be acting Sergeant. S/3971 L/Cpl S DILLON to be acting Corporal S/3232 L/Cpl E.H GREENWOOD to be Corporal (acting). All three, with pay attached to their rank. From Two Commenced at 9 p.m.	over
	17/2/17	9 a.m	Advance commenced to arrive at 9 a.m. in a constant stream of stretcher cases mostly sent until 11 p.m.. & British Officers and 140 other Ranks German Officers 2 and 14 Other Ranks passed through Main Dressing Station up to midnight. D.M.S. II Corps visited Main Dressing Station 11 a.m. 4-30 p.m Staff Sgt Elliott and thirty seven men moved to 2 Feet Tents for duty up the line. Capt Eagles R.amc at 11.45 proceeded to Bosque Headquarters in Station Valley and thence to Regimental Aid Post 1st R.m. Kt Lr. Given P A.D.M.S. visits M.D.S at 7-30 Then ambulances until 12 midnight	

Army Form C. 2118.

WAR DIARY
or
INTELLIGENCE SUMMARY.
(Erase heading not required.)

Place	Date	Hour	Summary of Events and Information	Remarks and references to Appendices
Lancs Dump	18/7/17	6pm	I was being A.D.M.S. Cpl Egerman and Eight bearers were detailed to proceed to Rifleman Post No R.A.L.1 to report to Capt Taylor R.A.M.C. for duty to assist in clearing Casualties from Sunken Road A.T.R.A.P. The day's wounded cases were cleared with great difficulty as the previous day's had been deeper and path outside immovable and very slippery Casualties passed through Main Dressing Station Trenchryck. 3 Officers/British and 45 Other Ranks. Work on the main Dressing Station was very heavy and constant as the casualties which passed through were Officers cases and severely wounded.	R.A.R.
Lancashire Dump	19/7/17	8pm	Casualties Officers 2. Other Ranks 14. Cpl Eagles R.A.M.C. returned from R.A.P. 1st R.W.F.	R.A.R.
LANCASHIRE DUMP	20/7/17		Casualties from 1 to 24th 1 Officer British and 20 Other Ranks. Received Operation Order Nº 77 and Nº 24.	R.A.R.

WAR DIARY or INTELLIGENCE SUMMARY

Army Form C. 2118.

Place	Date	Hour	Summary of Events and Information	Remarks and references to Appendices
LANCASHIRE DUMP	22/2/17	4pm	Casualties to midnight, nil Officers and 15 Other Ranks receiving D.A.D.M.S. Johnston under No. 24 R/2/2/17 took over the advanced dressing station and two posts from 2/2nd Ambulance 63rd R.D. Division. Relief completed upon Casualties Officers nil – Other Ranks 16.	
"	22/2/17	6pm	A.D.M.S. 63rd R.D. Division visited the Main Dressing Station. D.D.M.S. II Corps visited the Main Dressing Station. Capt PELLIER R.A.M.C. detailed from this Ambulance for duty as Regimental Medical Officer to the 4th Bn. Royal Fusiliers. The following men were marked to Military Medal for recent operations: S/3147 Pte M. CREMAN: S/3970 Pte W. BLANCHFLOWER: S/3543 Pte M. WILKINSON. S/3121. Pte REFWILD. Sixteen men under	
"	23/2/17		Casualties to midnight Officers nil Other Ranks 15. an N.C.O. sent up the line with relief	
"	24/2/17		Casualties to midnight Officers nil under Ranks 6.	
"	25/2/17		Casualties up to midnight Officers nil Other Ranks 11. Proceeded with D.A.D.M.S. to MIRAUMONT, over the ground recently gained with the object of finding suitable places for R.A.S. and Advanced Bearer Posts. There was very heavy shelling of approaches to MIRAUMONT. Got in to touch with the R.A.P's of the advancing Bats.	

Army Form C. 2118.

WAR DIARY
or
INTELLIGENCE SUMMARY.
(Erase heading not required.)

Place	Date	Hour	Summary of Events and Information	Remarks and references to Appendices
Lancashire Dump	26/1/17	6pm	Casualties to Midnight Officers 1 Other Ranks 24. Received ADMS Operation Order No 25. Established a forward bearer post at R 4 a 21. Map Ref Sheet 57 D S.E. and an advanced Dressing Station in R 8 a R 6 6 8 in PUSIEUX TRENCH. Capt GIBSON RAMC in charge this A.D.S. ADMS visited the Ambulance.	nil
Lancashire Dump	27/1/17	6pm	Casualties to midnight - 2 Officers and 24 Other Ranks. Received ADMS Operation Order No 26. Relief of the ADS and forward posts by 2/3 West Riding Field Ambulance Completed by 2 pm.	nil
LANCASHIRE DUMP	28/1/17	6pm	Lt R.T.TILLEY of this Ambulance has been awarded the Military Medal in connection with event November 13. D.M.S. 5th Army visited the main Dressing Station. Casualties :- 1 Officer and 17 Other Ranks.	nil

R.R.Tweedy Lieut. Col.
O.C. 1st/1st 7d RAMC
631 RM/D

MEDICAL.

CONFIDENTIAL

WAR DIARY

of

1st FIELD AMBULANCE

(3rd (R.N.) DIVISION.

From. 1st MARCH 1917.

To. 31st MARCH 1917.

R.S.C. Shute
Lieut. Colonel R.A.M.C.
O.C. 1st Fd Amb ce
63 (R.N.) Divn

Army Form C. 2118.

WAR DIARY
or
INTELLIGENCE SUMMARY.
(Erase heading not required.)

Place	Date	Hour	Summary of Events and Information	Remarks and references to Appendices
LANCASHIRE DUMP.	1/3/17	6pm	Casualties. Officers 1. O.R. nil. Capt LAVERICK. R.A.M.C. proceeded on 28/2/17 to NELSON Bn vice CAPT POWER R.A.M.C. admitted sick to Field Ambulance.	recd
"	2/3/17	6pm	Casualties Officers nil O.Ranks 1.	recd
"	3/3/17	6pm	Casualties Officers nil Other Ranks 11	recd
"	4/3/17	6pm	Casualties Officers nil Other Ranks 15	recd
"	5/3/17	6pm	Casualties Officers nil Other Ranks 5	recd
"	6/3/17	6pm	Casualties Officers nil Other Ranks 1. Party 91 h.c. & 20 men mining as working party for no 3 Coys	recd
"	7/3/17	6pm	no Casualties, battle, passed through.	ask
"	8/3/17	6pm	Casualties nil. The sick parade this morning reach the high total of 230. These were mostly from the Labour Companies 4 & 5 King's Liverpools.	ask

Army Form C. 2118.

WAR DIARY
or
INTELLIGENCE SUMMARY.
(Erase heading not required.)

Instructions regarding War Diaries and Intelligence Summaries are contained in F. S. Regs., Part II. and the Staff Manual respectively. Title pages will be prepared in manuscript.

Place	Date	Hour	Summary of Events and Information	Remarks and references to Appendices
Lancashire Dump	9/3/17	6pm	Casualties nil —	nil
	10/3/17	6pm	Casualties nil. Lt Colonel P.T.C. Robertson proceeded to England on 10 days leave. Capt Eagles took charge of the Unit. 50 men working with 54th T.A. returned to Lancashire Dump. O.C. 54 T.A. very pleased with the work they had done.	V Eagles
	11/3/17	6pm	Casualties — nil —	
	12/3/17	6pm	Casualties nil — Capt V.T.W. EAGLES. R.A.M.C awarded the Military Cross for work during recent operations.	V Eagles
	13/3/17	6pm	Capt F. IRWINE R.A.M.C joined the Ambulance for duty.	V Eagles
	14/3/17	6pm	Casualties Nil. 8/3194 Pte MAUNDRILL.C. awarded the D.C.M. work during recent operations.	V Eagles

WAR DIARY
or
INTELLIGENCE SUMMARY.

(Erase heading not required.)

Army Form C. 2118.

Place	Date	Hour	Summary of Events and Information	Remarks and references to Appendices
Lancashire Dump.	14/3/17	4	Capt. C.G. TIMMS R.A.M.C. Proceed to 7th/13th Bn Royal Fusiliers for duty permanently.	V Eagley
			O.C. Tent Sub Division Proceeded to the 3 CCS for duty. Capt IRVINE RAMC and Capt PELLIER RAMC in charge of party.	
	15/3/17		DDMS 2nd Corps inspected the ambulance on parade and delivered a congratulatory address to the men on their splendid work during recent active operations on the ANCRE. He also inspected the horse transport.	V Eagley
			Casualties nil -	V Eagley
	16/3/17		Casualties nil. O.C. 54th Field Ambulance visited & arrangements made with him for the handing over of Lancashire Dump to No 54 Field Ambulance.	V Eagley
	17/3/17			
WARLOY.	18/3/17.		In accordance with A.D.M.S. order the Ambulance moved to WARLOY. Transport horse in very poor condition. One Lancashire Dump opening found sheds left with the Mayor of WARLOY.	V Eagley

WAR DIARY
or
INTELLIGENCE SUMMARY.

(Erase heading not required.)

Army Form C. 2118.

Place	Date	Hour	Summary of Events and Information	Remarks and references to Appendices
HERISSART.	19/3/17	6 p.m.	The Ambulance moved to HERISSART. Capt PELLIER and Capt IRVINE. R.A.M.C. with 20 other ranks rejoined the Ambulance after completion of duty with 3 C.C.S. AVELUY.	V.Safy
BRETEL	20/3/17		The Ambulance moved to BRETEL. The roads to this place are very bad. Three Ambulances motor, done Sgt Swift A.S.C. did excellent work in extricating them from the mud. He was up all night working with them. Capt. IRVINE R.A.M.C. & two other ranks were dispatched to GEZAINCOURT to establish a subsidiary dressing Station here. B.H.Q. notified as to this alteration. One horse died of COLIC.	V.Safy
FORTEL	21/3/17		The Ambulance moved to FORTEL. Two horses left behind evacuated to C.C.S. Capt. IRVINE RAMC evacuated to C.C.S. with the Mayor.	V.Safy
GAUCHIN	22/3/17		The Ambulance moved to GAUCHIN. Six light draught horses joined the Ambulance. Lt Colonel Robertson R.A.M.C. returned from leave & rejoined the Ambulance.	Appx

Army Form C. 2118.

WAR DIARY
or
INTELLIGENCE SUMMARY.

(Erase heading not required.)

Instructions regarding War Diaries and Intelligence Summaries are contained in F. S. Regs., Part II. and the Staff Manual respectively. Title pages will be prepared in manuscript.

Place	Date	Hour	Summary of Events and Information	Remarks and references to Appendices
GAUCHIN.	23/3/17	6pm	Remained at rest in GAUCHIN for the day. Commanding Officers inspection at 2 pm.	AAR
CAUCHY A LA TOUR	24/3/17	6pm	The Ambulance moved to CAUCHY-A-LA-TOUR.	AAR
ST. HILAIRE	25/3/17	6pm	The Ambulance moved to ST. HILAIRE.	AAR
CALONNE-SUR-LA-LYS.	26/3/17	6pm	The Ambulance moved to CALONNE-SUR-LA-LYS. Two horses died of debility.	AAR
"	27/3/17	6pm	Rested for the day at CALONNE-SUR-LA-LYS.	AAR
"	28/3/17	6pm	Remained in CALONNE-SUR-LA-LYS. Training carried out in Squad drill Company drill and Physical Drill.	AAR

A.5834. Wt.W4973/M687 759,000 8/16 D.D. & L. Ltd. Forms/C.2118/13.

Army Form C. 2118.

WAR DIARY
or
INTELLIGENCE SUMMARY.
(Erase heading not required.)

Instructions regarding War Diaries and Intelligence Summaries are contained in F. S. Regs., Part II. and the Staff Manual respectively. Title pages will be prepared in manuscript.

Place	Date	Hour	Summary of Events and Information	Remarks and references to Appendices
LABOURSE	29/3/17	6 p.m.	The Ambulance moved to LABOURSE and arrived at 8 p.m. and took over buildings and billets occupied by 64 "Field Amb"	AAA
"	30/3/17	6 p.m.	Surgeon R.G. MORSAN. R.N. attached to this ambulance for instruction near ten other Ranks (reinforcements) joined the Ambulance for duty.	AAA
"	31/3/17	6 p.m.	Programme for training commenced	AAA

A.C.J.P. Mortimer.
Surg{?} Lt R.N.V.C.
O.C. 1st Fd Amb of
63 (R.N) Div{?}

A.584. Wt. W.4973/M687. 750,000. 8/16. D. D. & L. Ltd. Forms/C.2118/13.

No. 1. RN £ a.

B.E.F.

F.A.
SUMMARY OF MEDICAL WAR DIARIES FOR 1st R.N./63rd R.N. Divn. 13th Corps.

1st Army.

3rd Army from 11/4/17.

WESTERN FRONT April- May. '17.

O.C. Lt. Col. R. Robertson.

SUMMARISED UNDER THE FOLLOWING HEADINGS.

Phase "B" Battle of Arras- April- May. 1917.

1st Period Attack on Vimy Ridge (April.

2nd Period Capture of Siegfried Line May.

B.E.F.

F.A.
1st R.N./ 63rd R.N. Divn. WESTERN FRONT.
O.C. Lt. Col. R. Robertson. April. '17.
13th Corps 1st Army.
3rd Army from 11/4/17.

Phase "B" Battle of Arras- April- May. 1917.
1st Period Attack on Vimy Ridge April.

1917.	Headquarters. at Labourse.
April. 11th.	Moves: To Ourton with 188th Bde.
	Transfer. 3rd Army.
14th.	Moves: to X Hutments Ecoivres with 188th Bde.
22nd.	Moves Detachment: B.D. and 1 T.S.D. with transport to St. Catherine.
	Moves: To St. Catherine.
	2 S.Ds. at Maroeuil.
26th.	2 and "C" B.S.D. to A.D.S. 3rd Field Ambulance. Moves Detachment: "B" B.S.D. to A.D.S. 3rd F.A. 3 and 1 T.S.D. took over W.W. Dressing P. at Main Dressing Station St. Catherine.
	Casualties R.A.M.C. 0 and 2 wounded.
24th.	" " 0 and 2 wounded.
25th.	" " 0 and 1 killed 0 and 1 wounded.
27th.	Medical Arrangements: Charge of forward area for evacuation of sick and wounded taken over from 3rd Field Ambulance.
28th.	Operations. Zero hour 4.25.a.m. Attack commenced.
	Casualties Evacuation: 1st W. arrived at Advanced Dressing Station at 7 a.m. Constant and steady stream of wounded through day.
	Difficulty in collection of wounded due to strategical. position of ? Batln, heavy shelling, from machine guns and snipers. Special difficulties in regard to 1st R.M.L.I.

B.E.F.

<u>1st R.N., 63rd Divn.</u>   <u>WESTERN FRONT.</u>
O.C. Lt. Col. R. Robertson.   April. '17.
13th Corps, 3rd Army.

<u>Phase "B" cont.</u>
<u>1st Period cont.</u>

1917.
April. 30th.   <u>Moves:</u> To Maroeuil on relief by 93rd Field Ambulance.

Army Form C. 2118.

WAR DIARY
or
INTELLIGENCE SUMMARY.
(Erase heading not required.)

Instructions regarding War Diaries and Intelligence Summaries are contained in F. S. Regs., Part II. and the Staff Manual respectively. Title pages will be prepared in manuscript.

Place	Date	Hour	Summary of Events and Information	Remarks and references to Appendices
LA BOURSE	1-4-17	6pm	Visits the Advanced Dressing Station of 6" Division at VERMELLES with Surgeon Morgan (RN) for instruction.	MCR
"	2-4-17	6pm	G.O.C. of the Division visits this Ambulance.	MCR
"	3-4-17	6pm	Six reinforcements are posted to strengthen 9/the Ambulance. On unsurgical motor for 9 heavy draught and two light draught horses to complete establishment; only 4 light draught horses are available at the Remount Dept: that are not suitable for Field Ambulance as mules are in poor condition.	MCR
"	4-4-17	6pm	Ambulance Training	MCR
"	5-4-17	6pm	Ambulance Training	MCR
"	6-4-17	6pm	4 O.C. 1.S.S. Privates in this Ambulance; T/Capt J. Macpherson posts to C. Beaver Sub-Division one 7/Lieut L.A. Danson posts to B. Beaver Sub-Division.	MCR
"	7-4-17	6pm	Ambulance Training	MCR
"	8-4-17	6pm	"	MCR
"	9-4-17	6pm	Notified to be ready to move the Ambulance in 24 hours notice. Ambulance Training	MCR
"	10-4-17		Standing by to move in 24 hours.	MCR

Army Form C. 2118.

WAR DIARY
or
INTELLIGENCE SUMMARY.
(Erase heading not required.)

Instructions regarding War Diaries and Intelligence Summaries are contained in F.S. Regs., Part II. and the Staff Manual respectively. Title pages will be prepared in manuscript.

Place	Date	Hour	Summary of Events and Information	Remarks and references to Appendices
LA BOURSE	11/4/17	9 a.m.	Received orders from 154th Brigade to proceed with Brigade to OURTON.	AAR
OURTON	11/4/17	6 p.m.	Field Ambulance arrived at OURTON at 2.30 p.m.	AAR
"	12/4/17	6 p.m.	T/Capt J.B. FAIRCLOUGH. R.A.M.C. joined this Ambulance for duty and was posted to C Section Bearers.	AAR
"	13/4/17	6 p.m.	Field Ambulance awaiting orders to move	
"	14/4/17	10 a.m.	Field Ambulance received orders to march with Brigade to ECOIVRES.	AAR
X. HUTMENTS ECOIVRES	14/4/17	6 p.m.	Field Ambulance arrived at X. HUTMENTS, ECOIVRES at 5.30 p.m.	AAR
"	15/4/17	6 p.m.	T. Capt C. De C. PELLIER. R.A.M.C received orders to proceed to BOULOGNE to report to D.D.M.S. there for duty. Authority D.G.M.S. B/1483/168. D.9/4/17. Surg R.G. MORGAN. (R.N) proceeded to 3rd Field Amb 63 RND for temporary duty. Authority A.D.M.S. 7.3/152. ADMS Order No. 30 Received	AAR
"	16/4/17	6 p.m.	Ambulance Training	AAR
"	17/4/17	6 p.m.	Ambulance Training	AAR
"	18/4/17	6 p.m.	T. Capt M.A. POWER. R.A.M.C. reported this Ambulance for duty	AAR
"	19/4/17	6 p.m.	A.D.M.S. Order No. 31 Received & G.O.C. 154th Infy Brigade inspected Camp	AAR

ARMY FORM C.2118.

WAR DIARY

PLACE	DATE	HOUR	SUMMARY OF EVENTS AND INFORMATION	REMARKS AND REFERENCES TO APPENDICES
X HUTMENTS ECOIVRES	20/4/17	6 pm	Visited the forward area and returned forth in the line with all the team officers for instruction.	ACR
"	21/4/17	6 pm	Ambulance Training	ACR
"	22/4/17	7 pm	Received A.D.M.S. orders No. 128/153. D 22/4/17. The team division and one tent subdivision with the Transport proceed to ST. CATHERINES. Two tent subdivisions with the Transport and Transport Officer and Quarter Master proceeded to MAROEUIL and billeted with No 2 Coy. Divisional Train.	ACR
ST. CATHERINES	22/4/17	6 pm	The horse division and motor subdivision arrived 6 pm. The two Tent subdivisions arrived at MAROEUIL at 6 pm. Two Officers Capt. POWER. R.A.M.C. and Lt. DAVISON. R.A.M.C. and C. Bearer subdivision proceeded to A.D.S. of 3rd Field Ambulance.	ACR
"	23/4/17	6 pm	B. Bearer Subdivision proceeded to A.D.S. to report to 3rd Field Ambulance for duty. Capt. FAIRCLOUGH and 3 Officers, Capt. EAGLES. Capt. McGREGOR and one tent subdivision took over Charge of walking wounded dressing post at main dressing station ST. CATHERINES. No S/3999 Pte. BLAKELEY. No S/1366 Pte. BOARDMAN wounded, Pte BLAKELEY wounded carrying in the work(?)	ACR
"	24/4/17	6 pm	Visited A.D.S. & 3" Field Ambulance and M.D.S. No S/3606 Pte R. LEE. S/3939 Pte P. HIGGINS walking wounded dressing post at M.D.S. wounded	ACR
"	25/4/17	6 pm	No S/3753. Pte J.M. ENRIGHT time killed. No S/3614 Pte J. CLASPER wounded carrying in walking wounded dressing post at M.D.S.	ACR

ARMY FORM C 2118

WAR DIARY

PLACE	DATE	HOUR	SUMMARY OF INFORMATION AND EVENTS	REMARKS AND REFERENCES TO APPENDICES
ST. CATHERINES.	26/4/17	6 pm	Carrying on work of walking wounded post at M.D.S	nil
"	27/4/17	6 pm	Recvd orders from A.D.M.S. to take over charge of forward area for evacuation of sick and wounded from No. 3 Fwd Ambulance. Relief completed 8 pm.	nil
"	28/4/17	6 pm	Zero hour 4-25 am. attack commenced. First batch of wounded arrived at A.D.S. 7.30am. A constant and steady stream of wounded throughout all day long. Difficulty was experienced in collecting cases from the forward area owing to hostile shelling and heavy shelling and from machine guns & snipers. Difficulty was experienced in collecting cases from the front line.	nil
"	29/4/17	8 pm	6 casualties returned on forward area.	nil
"	30/4/17	8 pm	Capt. FAIRCLOUGH. R.A.M.C. and 1 N.C.O. and 2 O.R. proceeded to Sim Corps Stores. Duties for duty and are standing at the strength of this unit. Forward party of Fwd Amb. Unit moved to MAREUIL. Received Medical order A.D.M.S. No. 32. 93° Fwd Ambulance burned at A.D.S. to take over the lines worked by 312th & 63 Rd. Relief completed 8 pm.	nil

AC Richtater Major

(6392) Wt. W6192/P875 1,500,000 4/18 McA & W Ltd (E 2815) Forms W3091/4.   Army Form W.3091.

Cover for Documents.

Nature of Enclosures.

PATHOLOGY.

19. Pneumonia.

Notes, or Letters written.

MEDICAL

CONFIDENTIAL

WAR DIARY

1st FIELD AMBULANCE

63rd (RN) DIVISION

From 1st May 1917

To 31st May 1917

[Signature]
Lieut Col Lamb
O.C. 1st (RN) F.A.

B.E.F.

F.A.

SUMMARY OF MEDICAL WAR DIARIES FOR 1st R.N./63rd R.N. Divn. 13th Corps.

1st Army.

3rd Army from 11/4/17.

WESTERN FRONT April- May. '17.

O.C. Lt. Col. R. Robertson.

SUMMARISED UNDER THE FOLLOWING HEADINGS.

Phase "B" Battle of Arras- April- May. 1917.

1st Period Attack on Vimy Ridge (April.

2nd Period Capture of Siegfried Line May.

B.E.F.

1st R.N., 63rd R.N. Divn. WESTERN FRONT.
O.C. Lt. Col. R. Robertson. May. '17.
13th Corps, 3rd Army.

Phase "B" Battle of Arras- April- May. 1917.
2nd Period Capture of Siegfried Line May.

1917.
May. 1st.   Moves Detachment: B.D. and 1 T.S.D. rejoined
            Headquarters at Maroruil.

2nd.   Moves: To Frevillers.

9th.   "   " Cambligneul.

13th.   Decorations:-

            S/Sgt. N. Elliott   )
)
            Cpl. J.C. Green   ) awarded M.M. for operations
)
            Pte. Thorp.   ) Nov. 1916.

21st.   Moves: To St Catherine. Main Dressing Station
            and relieved 95th Field Ambulance.

25th.   Decorations. Cpl. Titley and Pte. Archibald awarded M.M.

31st.   Casualties. 19 and 237 wounded Total 21st-31st.

B.E.F.

<u>1st R.N., 63rd R.N. Divn.</u>   <u>WESTERN FRONT.</u>

<u>O.C. Lt. Col. R. Robertson.</u>   <u>May. '17.</u>

<u>13th Corps, 3rd Army.</u>

<u>Phase "B" Battle of Arras- April- May. 1917.</u>
<u>2nd Period Capture of Siegfried Line May.</u>

1917.

May. 1st.   <u>Moves Detachment:</u> B.D. and 1 T.S.D. rejoined Headquarters at Marœuil.

2nd.   <u>Moves:</u> To Frevillers.

9th.   "   " Cambligneul.

13th.   <u>Decorations:-</u>

     S/Sgt. N. Elliott)
)
     Cpl. J.C. Green) awarded M.M. for operations
)
     Pte. Thorp.) Nov. 1916.

21st.   <u>Moves:</u> To St Catherine. Main Dressing Station and relieved 95th Field Ambulance.

25th.   <u>Decorations</u> Cpl. Titley and Pte. Archibald awarded M.M.

31st.   <u>Casualties.</u> 19 and 237 wounded Total 21st-31st.

Army Form
C. 2118

WAR DIARY

Place	Date	Hour	Summary of Events and Information	Remarks and References to Appendices
MAROEUIL	1/5/17	6pm	The Advance and one tent subdivision arrived at MAROEUIL to join Reserve 9th Field Ambulance. Capt Pover Ramc.T.F. and Capt V. EAGLES. Mc Rame proceed on 14 days Special Leave.	acR
FRÉVILLERS	2/5/17	6pm	1st Field Ambulance marched from MAROEUIL to FREVILLERS and arrived 11pm. Surgeon R.G. MORGAN. R.N. detailed permanent for duty with 1st R.M. L.I. in accordance with ADMS order Nº 109/93. D. 30/4/17 and is struck off the strength of this Ambulance.	RcR
FREVILLERS	3/5/17	10am	Capt. F.R.H. LAVERICK Ramc.T.F. rejoined 1st Field Ambulance from NELSON. Bn. The following reinforcement joined 1st Field Ambulance for duty: Nº S/3431. Cpl J. GREEN. Nº S/3121 Pte R.E.F. WILD Nº S/3531. Pte E. HENDERSON. Nº S/3383 Pte J. HARBOTTLE Nº S/3192. Pte W.H. LEA. A.D.M.S and DA.Q.M.G visited this Ambulance Capt. F.R.H. LAVERICK. Ramc (T.F.) proceed to 63rd Div Train for Temporary duty. ADMS order Nº 73/9/3. D 2/5/17.	acR
FREVILLERS	4/6/17	6pm		acR

WAR DIARY

Place	Date	Hour	Summary of Events and Information	Remarks and Reference Appendices
FREVILLERS	5/5/17	6 pm	The following reinforcements were posted to:- No S/86 31. Cpl J. GREEN to C Bearer Subdivision: No S/3121. Pte R.F. WILD. No S/3531. Pte E. HENDERSON. No S/3383. Pte J. HARBOTTLE:- No S/3192. Pte W.H. LEA. to B Bearer Subdivision.	AACR
"	6/5/17	6 pm	Ambulance Training:- Ante typhoid inoculation in 17 Field Ambulance. HQ.	AAR
"	7/5/17	6 pm	Ambulance Training	AAR
"	8/5/17	9 pm	Ambulance Training. Received A.D.M.S. order F3/381. to move to CAMBLIGNEUL.	AAR
CAMBLIGNEUL	9/5/17	6 pm	Field Ambulance arrived CAMBLIGNEUL. 11 a.m. The following promotions were approved. Authority A.D.M.S. 5/35. and to take effect from 5/5/17. No S/3036. Cpl J. HOLMES to be acting Sgt:- No S/3583. L/Cpl W. TITLEY to A/Cpl:- No S/3194. Pte C. MAUNDRILL to A/L Cpl with pay. No S/3786 A/RQM H. CROSWELL to R/Sgt Substantial	AACR
"	10/5/17	6 pm	Lt + Qm WILLIAMS granted leave of absence from 12 May to 22 May. A.D.M.S. notes this statement.	AAR

Army Form
C 2118

WAR DIARY

PLACE	DATE	HOUR	SUMMARY OF EVENTS AND INFORMATION	REMARKS AND REFERENCES TO APPENDICES
CAMBLIGNEUL	11/5/17	6 p.m.	Training of Ambulance.	R.C.R.
"	12/5/17	6 p.m.	Temporary Surgeon D.L. BAXTER R.N. joined this Ambulance for duty and training	R.C.R.
"	13/5/17	6 p.m.	Presentation by Military Medals by Major Fenton Laurie to 63rd R.N.D. awarded for Ambulance 13th F.A. Gazettes No. N.o.S/33 to S.Sgt. N. ELLIOTT. No.S/3443.1 Cpl. J.C. GREEN No.S/3694 Pte A.W. THORP. Capt. F.R.H. LAVERICK R.A.M.C. T. rejoined this Ambulance for duty	R.C.R.
"	14/5/17	6 p.m.	No. 144102. A/Sgt Major J.W. RANFORD. R.A.M.C. appointed to this Ambulance. Authority A.D.M.S. No. 150/46.D. 14/5/17	R.C.R.
"	15/5/17	6 p.m.	Training of Ambulance	R.C.R.
"	16/5/17	6 p.m.		R.C.R.
"	17/5/17	6 p.m.	Capt Eagle & Capt Power Rame returned from leave.	R.C.R.
"	18/5/17	6 p.m.		R.C.R.
"	19/5/17	6 p.m.		R.C.R.
"	20/5/17	6 p.m.	Capt MacGregor Rame & one N.C.O. & three O.R.'s recce'd to Ste CATHERINES before our M.D.S. taking over 96 Field R.C.R.	R.C.R.

WAR DIARY

Army Form C 2118

Place	Date	Hour	Summary of Events and Information	Remarks and References to Appendices
ST. CATHERINES	21/5/17	6 pm	7 Field Ambulance left CAMBIGNEUL 7am and arrived at ST. CATHERINES at 11am and took over the M.D.S. from 75th Amb. Wounded admissions:- Officers nil. Other Ranks. 16.	A.C.R.
"	22/5/17	6 pm	Wounded Admissions:- Officers nil. Other Ranks 12. Major General Lawie G.O.C. 63rd R.N.D. visited the Main Dressing Station	A.C.R.
"	23/5/17	6 pm	Wounded Admissions:- 2 Officers and 11 Other Ranks.	A.C.R. R.C.R.
"	24/5/17	6 pm	Wounded Admissions:- Officers nil. 14 Other Ranks.	R.C.R.
"	25/5/17	6 pm	Wounded Admissions:- Officers 3 ; 30 Other Ranks. No S/3538 Cpl. TITLEY. W and No S/3322 Pte. ARCHIBALD. J.D. awarded Military Medals	R.C.R.
"	26/5/17	6 pm	Wounded Admissions:- Officers 3. Other Ranks 30. 7 F.R. granted leave to England	R.C.R.
"	27/5/17	6 pm	Wounded Admissions:- Officers 3 ; Other Ranks 24.	R.C.R.
"	28/5/17	6 pm	Wounded Admissions:- Officers 3 : Other Ranks. 36. ; 3 Other Ranks granted leave to England for ten days.	R.C.R.
"	29/5/17	6 pm	Wounded Admissions:- 3 Officers 9. & 42 Other Ranks.	R.C.R.
"	30/6/17	6 pm	Wounded Admissions:- Officers nil. 16 Other Ranks; Officers nil	R.C.R.
"	31/5/17	6 pm	Wounded Admissions ; 2 Officers & 6 Other Ranks. 5 a.m. S XIII Corps including the Divn. Dressing Stations 16 Other Ranks granted leave to England. T/Capt CANT. F.Y. Lau to this Amb. from	R.C.R. R.C.R.

MEDICAL

= WAR DIARY =

CONFIDENTIAL

- of -

1st (R.N) Field Ambulance
63rd (R.N) Division

- from -

1st June 1917 to 30th June 1917

COMMITTEE FOR THE
MEDICAL HISTORY OF THE WAR
Date — 7 AUG. 1917

1ST
FIELD AMBULANCE,
63RD (R.N.) DIVISION.
No................
Date 1/7/17.

Lieut-Col RAMC
Commanding

WAR DIARY
or
INTELLIGENCE SUMMARY.

Army Form C. 2118.

Place	Date	Hour	Summary of Events and Information	Remarks and references to Appendices
ST. CATHERINES	1/6/17	6 p.m.	Wounded admitted:- Officers nil. Other Ranks. 12.	nil
"	2/6/17	6 p.m.	Wounded admitted:- Officers nil. Other Ranks. 20.	nil
"	3/6/17	6 p.m.	Wounded admitted:- Officers 1. Other Ranks. 25. Capt. T. R. K. LAVERICK proceeded to ST. OMER for duty and was struck off the strength of this Ambulance; post ADMS. 10g/110. dated 3/6/17. Capt. M.A.P. WEIR proceeded to H.A.C. 13th for temporary duty;- nine Other Ranks granted leave to England from 3/6/17 to 18/6/17	nil
"	4/6/17	6 p.m.	Wounded admissions:- Officers. 1. Other Ranks. 22.	nil
"	5/6/17	6 p.m.	Wounded admissions:- Officers 1. Other Ranks 26.:- Three Other Ranks reinforcements joined for duty.	nil
"	6/6/17	6 p.m.	Wounded admissions:- Officers nil; Other Ranks 11.	nil
"	7/6/17	6 p.m.	Wounded admissions:- Officers nil; Other Ranks 17.; 16 Other Ranks granted leave to England from 7 # 7.9 June :- The A.A-QMG 2nd Army inspected this Ambulance.	nil
"	8/6/17	6 p.m.	Wounded admissions:- Officers 2. includes Major General HEATH. C.E. of 2nd Army:- Other Ranks 18.	nil
"	9/6/17	6 p.m.	Wounded admissions:- Officers 2. Other Ranks. 30.	nil
"	10/6/17	6 p.m.	Wounded admissions:- Officers nil.; Other Ranks 3.	nil

Army Form C. 2118.

WAR DIARY
or
INTELLIGENCE SUMMARY.

(Erase heading not required.)

Instructions regarding War Diaries and Intelligence Summaries are contained in F. S. Regs., Part II. and the Staff Manual respectively. Title pages will be prepared in manuscript.

Place	Date	Hour	Summary of Events and Information	Remarks and references to Appendices
ST. CATHERINES	11/6/17	6 p.m.	Proceeded Ambucairie. Officers nil. Other Ranks 3.	nil
CAMBLIGNEUL	12/6/17	6 p.m.	Ambulance moved to CAMBLIGNEUL. In Other Ranks proceeded on leave to England. Routine Parades.	nil
"	13/6/17	6 p.m.	Surg. BAXTER. (R.N) proceeded to Home B⁰ for temporary duty	nil
"	14/6/17	6 p.m.	Routine Parades.	nil
"	15/6/17	6 p.m.	Capt. E. M. DUNLOP. RAMC (T.F) joined the Ambulance for duty and is taken on strength of England. Capt. Power. Ramc. proceeded to	nil
"	16/6/17	6 p.m.	1 Other Ranks granted leave to England. 1 Other Ranks proceeded to Home B⁰ for temporary duty. Auth. A/Adm.S. #9/30 dated 15/6/17. Capt CRAIG Ramc proceeded to Hospital of Enghien for examination of Expert Leucillis for improving duty. 10 days	nil
"	17/6/17	6 p.m.	Capt CANT. Ramc. proceeded to Paris Guerliss for improving duty.	nil
"	18/6/17	6 p.m.	Lt Col. R.T.C. Robertson R.A.M.C. S.P. proceeded on leave to England. Capt V. T. W. Eagle R.A.M.C took over Command of the Ambulance. Capt J. Mac Gregor R.A.M.C reported the Ambulance for duty. Capt/Mac Gregor R.A.M.C reported the Ambulance for duty ex the Paris leave. T. Surgeon Cunningham. V.Mr.S. R.N. rejoined the Ambulance for duty.	V.M.S

WAR DIARY
or
INTELLIGENCE SUMMARY.

Army Form C. 2118.

Place	Date	Hour	Summary of Events and Information	Remarks and references to Appendices
CAMBLIGNEUL	19th	6pm	T/15931. A/SSM. T. HARMAN. A.S.C. reverts to his permanent rank C.Q.M.S. and reports to No 3 Coy. Div Train for duty. T/14189 A/SSM. J.M GREGGAINS A.S.C joined this unit on the 18th instant for duty. Routine parades	1.M.E.
"	20th	6pm	Routine parades	1.7.W.E
"	21st	6pm	Routine parades. Capt Power RAMC rejoined this unit from detached duty with H.O.D.B.	1.7.W.E
	22nd	6pm	Routine parades. Capt Cant RAMC rejoined this unit from detached duty with 5th Royal Fusiliers	1.M.E.
	23rd		The following Other Ranks proceeded on 10 days leave to England. T/Surgeon Cunningham M.C R.N. S/3506 Pte HOPPER.C S/3964 Pte Donoghty W.H. S/3982 Pte GWYTHER.J.W S/3686 Pte PILKINGTON. S/2295 Pte NICHOLSON.G. S/2204 Pte JOHNSTON.R A.D.M.S treated and inspected this Ambulance. Punishment Awards. S/2309 Pte ANDERSON.D on Train. "Absent without leave". Forfeits 1 days pay under Royal Warrant	1.M.E.

WAR DIARY
or
INTELLIGENCE SUMMARY.
(Erase heading not required.)

Army Form C. 2118.

Place	Date	Hour	Summary of Events and Information	Remarks and references to Appendices
CAMBLIGNEUL	24th	6pm	Routine parades. Capt DUNLOP. E.M. R.A.M.C. proceeded on Temporary duty to Anson Bn 25th Xc following other ranks granted	V.M.S
	25th	6pm	10 days to England from 26th to 6th July. S/3976. Pte C.L. HARDMAN. S/2054 Pte WHITE.J. S/4067 Pte DITCHBURN.A. S/4010 Pte WILSON.A. S/4160 Pte LEES.H. S/4167 Pte MORRIS.A. S/4033 Pte WILD.W.A. S/4031 Pte WALMSLEY.G.H. S/4007 Pte ROBSON.J.N. An Engine draught & one heavy draught horse received taken on strength.	V.M.S
	26th	6pm	Routine Parades.	V.M.S
	27th	6pm	D.D.M.S. XIII Corps visited & inspected this unit. Routine parade. One light draught Dark Bay Horse left behind by the 146 Field Ambulance broke its leg in the night of 26/27 & had to be destroyed this morning. C.O. carriers notified.	V.M.S
	28th	6pm	Routine parades. four Brig Motor Am Carriers proceeded to S/Sgt THORPE S for duty with M.A.C.	V.M.S
	29th	6pm	Routine parade.	V.M.S

WAR DIARY
or
INTELLIGENCE SUMMARY.

Army Form C. 2118.

(Erase heading not required.)

Place	Date	Hour	Summary of Events and Information	Remarks and references to Appendices
CAMBLIGNEUIL	30/6/17	5pm	Three Other ranks granted leave to England from 2 July to 11 July. Lt. Col. R.T.C. Robertson returned from ten days leave of absence to England.	Recd

A.E.C. Robertson

63RD DIVISION

NO. 148TH (RN) FLD AMBULANCE

~~JLY 1917-DEC 1918~~

1916 JUN — 1919 APL

CONFIDENTIAL.

WAR DIARY.

of

No 148. (Royal Naval) Field Ambulance

63rd.(R.N.) D.

From   1st.July

To.   31st.July.1917.

[signature]
Lieut.-Col., R.A.M.C.,
Commanding 148th. (R.N.) FIELD AMB.

COMMITTEE FOR THE MEDICAL HISTORY OF THE WAR — Date 10 SEP. 1917

WAR DIARY or INTELLIGENCE SUMMARY

Army Form C. 2118.

Place	Date	Hour	Summary of Events and Information	Remarks and references to Appendices
CAMBLIGNEUL	1/7/17	6 pm	Routine Parades:- Three Other Ranks Grades have to England. No. 14402 A/Sgt Major J. RANFORD reverted to his permanent rank of Staff Sgt under K.R. para 597 on 30/6/17.	RCR
"	2/7/17	6 pm	Visited the forward Area with the D.A.D.M.S. - Routine Parades. Punishments:- No. S/3524 Pte. R. EMERSON award Reverted to rank of Private for following offence: Conduct to the prejudice of good order & military discipline in that he proceeded duty at inspection. No. S/3694 Pte. W. WOODEN. A.S.C. absent without leave from 4-20am to 6-45am on 27/6/17 awarded 7 days No.2 Field Punishment and forfeits 1 day's pay under R. Warrant. No. S/2263 Pte. T. CRONARTY. A.S.C. absent without leave from 7-20am to 6pm on 27/6/17 awarded 7 days No. 2 Punishment & forfeits 1 days pay under R.W. No. S/1880 Pte. T.H. WEST awarded 7 days No. 2 F.P. & forfeits 1 days pay under R.W. Received Standing Order No. 30 ADMS 2/4/17	RCR
ANZIN	3/7/17	6 pm	Field Ambulance HQrs arrived 10 a.m. - took over the following stations from the 9/5- Field Ambulance in the forward area. Being Completely equipped. Advanced Dressing Station at H.1 - c. 3. 8 and evacuating Posts. B. 28. a. 58. at the 2/ N. RTS (H.d. Q.5.) and B.13 N. Central Punishment. No. S/3993 Pte. S. CLARKE absent without leave from 6.30 am. 29/6/17 to 6.30 am. 30/6/17. Award 7 days No 2 F. Punishment & forfeits 2 days pay under R. Warrant	RCR
"	4/7/17	6 pm	Took over in the forward Area from the 3" Division (the "Lowland") this Sector on the left of 63rd R.N.D. to PRINCESS Trench in 3 Division. Location of Regimental Aid Posts. B.11.a. 5.8 and B.17.c. 3.0. hospital Shell 51 B.N.W. and Aleijont B.16. c. 6.6	RCR

Army Form C. 2118.

WAR DIARY
or
INTELLIGENCE SUMMARY.
(Erase heading not required.)

Place	Date	Hour	Summary of Events and Information	Remarks and references to Appendices
ANZIN	4/7/17	6pm	A new Relay post was formed by me at B.15.d.Y.6. that S1.B.Y.W. also a clearing post at B.21.C.7.5. in the Railway Cutting. Relief of 3rd Division No 14 Field Ambulance completed by 6pm.	ack
"			A/Sgt Major W.A. CLENSHAW. RAMC reported for duty as A/Sgt Major of this Field Ambulance in Relay on Staff Sgt S. RANFORD, RAMC. Authority DDMS No 569. dated 3/7/17	ack
"	5/7/17	8pm	Staff Sgt J. RANFORD proceeded to No 15 Field Ambulance for duty. T/Surg CUNNINGHAM (R.N) reported his return from leave to England.	
"	6/7/17	6pm	T/Surg CUNNINGHAM (R.N) posted to HAWKE Batt and to take up the Strength of this Unit. Authority A.D.M.S. No 109/13.8 dated 5/7/17. Capt DUNLOP RamGT? rejoined this Ambulance from detached duty with Anson Bass.	ack
"	7/7/17	6pm	Collecting and Evacuating, Sick and wounded from forward area. This is promptly done by the Light Railway running from B.21.C.7-5 to ST CATHERINES, M.D. Station. two other ranks granted leave to England.	ack
"	8/7/17	6pm	Collecting and evacuating wounded from the forward area.	ack
"	9/7/17	6pm	" " " " " " " Two other Ranks granted leave to England.	ack

(AP190). Wt. W1283g/M1293. 75,000. 1/17. D.D. & L., Ld. Forms/C.2118.t4.

WAR DIARY or INTELLIGENCE SUMMARY

Army Form C. 2118.

Place	Date	Hour	Summary of Events and Information	Remarks and references to Appendices
ANZIN	10/7/17	6 a.m.	Collecting and Evacuating wounded from the forward area	nil
"	11/7/17	6 a.m.	Special Parade 9.30 a.m. "Gas Inspection Kit"	nil
"	12/7/17	6 a.m.	Collecting & Evacuating wounded from the forward area	nil
"	13/7/17	6 a.m.	" " " " " "	nil
"	14/7/17	6 a.m.	" " " " " "	nil
"	15/7/17	6 p.m.	" " " " " " Over the Kent Sports came off	nil
"	16/7/17	6 a.m.	Collecting & Evacuating wounded from the forward area. Inspection of Motor Air Transport of this Ambulance by A.D.M.S. Divisional Train in accordance with A.F.S. order No. 35/259 of 13/7/17. Handed over Regimental Aid Post B.11.d.6.8 and Relay Post B.16 b Central 3 & Relay S1.6 N.W. to an Officer of "B" (W) Field Ambulance 5th Division. Relief completed at 6 p.m.	nil
"	17/7/17	9 p.m.	Collecting & Evacuating Wounded = Ambulance Trolley having completed and running on light railway between BAILLEUL and ST CATHERINES Main Dressing Station.	nil
"	18/7/17	6 p.m.	Reciev'd of Forward area by No.3 F. Ambulance and Completed by 6 p.m. in accordance with A.D.M.S. order No. 40. Dated 16/7/17. Received Evacuation order A.F orders No.41. Oct 15/7/17. The following number has been assigned to 2nd Field Ambulance. No. 148. Auth. A.C.I. N°1046. Dated 3/7/17	nil

Army Form C. 2118.

WAR DIARY
or
INTELLIGENCE SUMMARY.
(Erase heading not required.)

Instructions regarding War Diaries and Intelligence Summaries are contained in F. S. Regs., Part II. and the Staff Manual respectively. Title pages will be prepared in manuscript.

Place	Date	Hour	Summary of Events and Information	Remarks and references to Appendices
ANZIN	19/7/17	6pm	Routine Parade	nil
"	20/7/17	6pm	Routine Parade. Capt. DUNLOP. RAMC new portn temporarily as 2i/c D/E 14 "Hoosiers" Regiment	nil
"	21/7/17	6pm	Capt. CANT. RAMC was posted for temporary duty to NELSON Bn. Routine Parade.	nil
"	22/7/17	4pm	1 x Cpl and 15 men proceed to XIII Corps Rest Station. Capt. J.C. DOWSE. RAMC posted to this Ambulance and taken on its strength and attached to A.D.M.S. Staff for duty. A.D.M.S. N⁰ 09/142 Routine Parade.	nil
"	23/7/17	6pm	Routine Parade	nil
"	24/7/17	6pm	Routine Parade	nil
"	25/7/17	6pm	Routine Parade	nil
"	26/7/17	—	Capt. Hincksman RAMC detailed for temporary duty in another Army Area.	nil
"	27/7/17	6pm	Ramc Sgts. Whi Field Ambulance and Presentation of Purse by 20 NC 63"RND	nil
"	28/7/17	6pm	Routine Parade.	nil
"	29/7/17	9pm	Lieut. H. DAW. RAMC joined this Ambulance for duty and was posted to A section.	nil
"	30/7/17	10pm	Capt. DUNLOP. RAMC posted permanently to 14 "Worcester" B⁻ and to labour Bn 16 "Shursts" Amb. A.D.M.S. N⁰ 709/14.5 of 28/7/17. Routine Parade	nil
"	31/7/17	10pm	D.M.S.'s tany inspected inspected Ambulance twice. Deep and Construct by the Ambulance tor not Performances covered from the Forward Area. Victor 5 Threshed Grant N⁰ 42	nil

A.H. Robinson
Lt Col

CONFIDENTIAL.   MEDICAL.

WAR DIARY of the

148th (Royal Naval) FIELD AMBULANCE.

For the period 1st to 31st AUGUST 1917.

31:8:17.

Lieut.-Col. R.A.M.C.
Commanding 148th (R.N.) Field Amb.
63rd (R.N.) Division.

Army Form C. 2118.

WAR DIARY
or
INTELLIGENCE SUMMARY.
(Erase heading not required.)

Place	Date	Hour	Summary of Events and Information	Remarks and references to Appendices
ANZIN	1/8/17	6pm	Took over the charge of the forward area and took over from 150 (RN) F. Amb. relief completed at 8pm. Capt. C. Johnson Rame S.P.	nil
"	2/8/17	6pm	Capt Johnson posted to Walking post at Rly D.O.S. (Shaft 5; 8 RW) for instruction in the work of the forward area under Capt Don Rame.	nil
"	3/8/17	6pm	Collecting and Evacuating wounded from the forward area. Capt (Cant Rame) ranks from Wilson 8am	nil
"	4/8/17	6pm	Three Other Ranks Granted ten days leave to England.	nil
"	5/8/17	6pm	Capt. Cant Rame attended the Commanders Parade Service	nil
"	6/8/17	6pm	Enemy Gas Shell attack at GIVENCHY at 3 a.m. 35 Cases were evacuated to MDS Three deaths took place at C.Post 14 & D.O.S.	nil
"	7/8/17	6pm	Collecting and Evacuating from the forward area	nil
"	8/8/17	6pm	3.0 p.m. Lt. Col. W. Sharp interviewed Cq. 9,10 & 188 Infty Brigades as to Stretcher bearers in communication trenches.	nil
"	"	4pm	Interview at 7pm. S. office with reference to Gas(shell)	nil
"	9/8/17	6pm	Capt. F.P. Cant Rame proceeded to England (Bristol) to hear office on completion of contract	nil
"	10/8/17	6pm	Capt. V.T.W. EAGLES admitted to M.D.S. Sick and Evacuated to No 30 C.C.S Capt Johnson and Lieut Daw attached to 149 F.D. Amb. for Temporary duty	nil

Army Form C. 2118.

WAR DIARY
or
INTELLIGENCE SUMMARY.
(Erase heading not required.)

Instructions regarding War Diaries and Intelligence Summaries are contained in F.S. Regs., Part II. and the Staff Manual respectively. Title pages will be prepared in manuscript.

Place	Date	Hour	Summary of Events and Information	Remarks and references to Appendices
ANZIN	10/9/17	6pm	Capt Reid and Capt Clarke Renou returned from 149"/75 that for training area duty with the Ambulance in the training area. Capt M.A. POWER placed in charge of the forward area via Capt Pughe evacuating sick.	nil
"	11/9/17	6pm	Other Ranks proceeded on leave to England. Evacuation of sick and wounded from forward area	nil
"	12/9/17	6pm	Evacuation of sick and wounded from forward area.	nil
"	13/9/17	6pm	Two other Ranks sent to 1st Army Rest Camp	nil
			Received A.D.M.S. Can No 43. dated 13/9/17	
"	14/9/17	6pm	Handed over charge of the forward area to 150" RN.Field Ambulance Another reinforcement arrived from the base. B. Section opening dressing Station at ANZIN for reception of local sick Capt Johnson Reid and Lieut Dew Renou attached to 150 & amb for temporary duty	nil
"	15/9/17	6pm		nil
"	16/9/17	6pm	86/3916 Pte Ashworth.H. to XIII Corps School of Sanitation for instruction	nil
"	17/9/17	6pm		nil
"	18/9/17	6pm	Three Other Ranks proceeded on leave to England	nil

Army Form C. 2118.

WAR DIARY
or
INTELLIGENCE SUMMARY.
(Erase heading not required.)

Place	Date	Hour	Summary of Events and Information	Remarks and references to Appendices
ANZIN	19/9/17	6pm	Other Ranks granted leave to England:- No. S/314 S. Pte. Ford. T. & 750 Pte Piuk. and No. S/346 Pte Murray R. & 148 (R.N.) 2nd Lieut for duty.	A.C.I.R
"	20/9/17	6pm	Routine Parades.	A.C.I.R
"	21/9/17	6pm	Routine Parades.	A.C.I.R
"	22/9/17	6pm	Lieut D&W Ramie T.C. reported from hospital duty with 150 (RN) School	A.C.I.R
"	23/9/17	6pm	Routine parades	A.C.I.R
"	24/9/17	6pm	Routine parades	A.C.I.R
"	25/9/17	6pm	Other Ranks granted leave to England:- Four reinforcements arrived from the Base viz Coy Sgt Major SSM and two Privates on the strength of the Bn	A.C.I.R
"	26/9/17	6pm	Capt Johnson C. Rawe. A. posted to duty with the 2nd Bn Hertford Rifles and was struck off the strength of the unit	A.C.I.R
"	27/9/17	6pm	Commenced erecting Huers huts for personnel at ANZIN. (one standing completed) and commenced work on standing for Horses.	A.C.I.R
"	28/9/17	6pm	Received from H.M.S. Stratton No. 616. 1st Pte Oer. Chalk. Pte Forward over for transmission of Syf received from the 150/29 Aust. Army Corp Base at 8pm R.A.P.S	A.C.I.R
"	29/9/17	8pm	Cpl Jackson all the Armourers Forth in the Repair Section drew the R.A.P.S	A.C.I.R

WAR DIARY
or
INTELLIGENCE SUMMARY

Army Form C. 2118.

Place	Date	Hour	Summary of Events and Information	Remarks and references to Appendices
AIZIN	30/9/17	6pm	NB 5/30 63. St Thatcher. S.H. posted to 150 (RN) FD Amb. to duty.	AAR
"	31/9/17	6pm	Evacuation of Sick & Wounded from 2nd Provd Bn.	AAR

A.C.R...........
LIEUT.-COLONEL, R.A.M.C.
COMMANDING 1st (R.N.) FIELD AMBULANCE.

MEDICAL.   C.O.N.F.I.D.E.N.T.I.A.L.

W-A-R   D-I-A-R-Y

of

148th (Royal Naval) FIELD AMBULANCE

for the period.

1st. September 1917 to 30th. September 1917 ; inclusive.

COMMITTEE FOR THE
MEDICAL HISTORY OF THE WAR
Date — 5 NOV. 1917

Lieut.-Col., R.A.M.C.,
Commanding 148th (R.N.) Field Ambulance.

Army Form C. 2118.

WAR DIARY
or
INTELLIGENCE SUMMARY.
(Erase heading not required.)

Instructions regarding War Diaries and Intelligence Summaries are contained in F.S. Regs., Part II. and the Staff Manual respectively. Title pages will be prepared in manuscript.

Place	Date	Hour	Summary of Events and Information	Remarks and references to Appendices
ANZIN	1/9/17	6pm	Evacuation of Sick & Wounded from the Forward area.	nil
"	2/9/17	6pm	Evacuation of Sick & Wounded from Forward area. ADMS Junction order No. 46 Received.	nil
"	3/9/17	6pm	ADMS Junction order No. 65 D 2/9/17 recieved. Relief completed by 6pm.	nil
"	4/9/17	6pm	Evacuation of Forward area	nil
"	5/9/17	6pm	Capt. DAVID G.O.N.J. RAMC to joined this Ambulance for duty. No. 5/3 5743 Pte WILKINSON M. and No. 6/3148 Pte CREHAN N. 57758 M.C. Coy for rear duties and as stretcher off the Strength of this Ambulance.	nil
MAROEUIL	6/9/17	6pm	Took over the Dressing Station and toiveting accommodation at MAROEUIL from the 9.5 Yr Ambt 31st Division. Relief completed at 6pm	nil
"	7/9/17	6pm	No. 6/3972 Pte SKILLING A evacuated Sick to No. 30 C.C.S.	nil
"	8/9/17	6pm	1st Lieut. DOW J.N. US MORC. and 1st Lieut. PIERCE W.J. US.MORC. posted to this Ambulance for duty and temporarily attached to 14.9th (RN) Fd Amb. No. M/339073 Pte CONWAY.J.A.S.C.M.T. posted to this unit for duty.	nil
"	9/9/17	6pm	Evacuation of Sick and Wounded	nil
"	10/9/17	6pm	Evacuation new ADMS No. 48 rec'd	nil
"	11/9/17	6pm	Capt. DAVIDSON. RAMC detailed to take Sick parade The Hood Bn	nil
"	12/9/17	6pm	Relief of 148 (RN) Fd Amb by 16 D (RN) Fd Amb in the Forward area Completed by 6pm.	nil
"	13/9/17	6pm	Routine parades	nil

WAR DIARY
or
INTELLIGENCE SUMMARY.

Army Form C. 2118.

Place	Date	Hour	Summary of Events and Information	Remarks and references to Appendices
MAROEUIL	14/9/17	6 pm	Routine Passion - 9 Cpl DILLON. J. revert to L/Cpl with effect from 25/8/17 -	RAK
"	15/9/17	6 pm	Capt. DAWSON. J. proc temporarily to Command A. Suton and Lieut DAW H. to B Sector. Two other ranks granted leave to England.	RAK
"	16/9/17	6 pm	Capt. V. T. W. EAGLES. M.C. RAMC evacuated sick and is struck off the strength of this unit. Authority A.D.M.S. N° 109/5/6. d. 15/9/17	RAK
"	17/9/17	6 pm	N° 5/2637 Pte SAUNDERS. E. and N° 5/3531 Pte HENDERSON. N. E. and N° 5/3735 Pte ROWLANDS. A. awarded 28 days Field Punishment N° 1. For offence: Lieut DAW RAMC attached for temporary duty with 3 R.S.F.T.	RAK
"	18/9/17	6 pm	Routine Person -	RAK
"	19/9/17	6 pm	" " "	
"	20/9/17	5 pm	Lieut DOW F.S.R. and Lieut PIERCE J.S.R. report for duty on completion of temporary duty with 149 th (R.N.) Bo Amb.	RAK
"	21/9/17	6 pm	Capt DAVIDSON. J. RAMC detailed to report to D.M.S & Army for duty	RAK
"	22/9/17	6 pm	Recd A.D.M.S. Circular order N° 49.	RAK
"	22/9/17	6 pm	This Unit relieved by London Feild Ambulance and renewed from Sector (23 Sept - 3 Oct) and route Camp Powex R. Lamé gave to a days leave in England. The Unit moved to AVERDOING (in motor buses and transport by road)	RAK
AVERDOING	23/9/17	6 pm	Received F.S.R. Part 1 order (BM 600) and moved to HOUVELIN by road	RAK

WAR DIARY
or
INTELLIGENCE SUMMARY.

Army Form C. 2118.

(Erase heading not required.)

Place	Date	Hour	Summary of Events and Information	Remarks and references to Appendices
HOUVELIN	24/9/17	6pm	Routine Parades and Fatigues for cleaning up Billets.	Nil
"	25/9/17	6pm	G.O.C. 188 Infantry Brigade visited the Ambulance	Nil
"	26/9/17	6pm	Cleaning up billets and improving the Camouflage Curtains of our occupied of this Ambulance	Nil
"	27/9/17	6pm	Found Programme of training from A.D.M.S. for 27.28.29 September. Commenced Programme of training - carried out routine march from 6.30 to 7.30 p.m. with all ranks of the Ambulance wearing box respirators	Nil
"	28/9/17	6pm	Routine Parades & Training	Nil
"	29/9/17	6pm	Routine Parades & Training. Kiroupstal Lieut Williams RN granted leave to return to England from 30/9/17 to 10/10/17	Nil
"	30/9/17	6pm	Pm MO and 76 Thun other rank returned from AVBIGNY on completing temporary duty with SM Corps Rest Station. Lieut DAW RAMC returned to this unit from temporary duty with 2. R.M.L.I.	Nil

R.C.R. Pinkerton
LIEUT.-COLONEL, R.A.M.C.
COMMANDING 1st (R.N.) FIELD AMBULANCE.

MEDICAL.   CONFIDENTIAL.

WAR   DIARY
of
148th (R.N.) Field Ambulance
for period,

1st. October, 1917 to   31st. October 1917.

[Stamp: COMMITTEE FOR THE MEDICAL HISTORY OF THE WAR Date -8 DEC. 1917]

Lieut.-Col., R.A.M.C.,
Commanding 148th (R.N.) Field Ambulance.

WAR DIARY or INTELLIGENCE SUMMARY

Army Form C. 2118.

(Erase heading not required.)

Place	Date	Hour	Summary of Events and Information	Remarks and references to Appendices
HOUTKERQUE	1/10/17	6 p.m.	Routine Parades and Fatigues. Received A.D.M.S. order No. 123/23 0/3 dated 30/9/17. Received No. 375 & 4/13/1/A. Dated 30/9/17 from 63rd R.N.D.	NIL
" "	2/10/17	6 p.m.	Capt T.W. CLARKE R.A.M.C. posted to this unit "undertaken for duty from XIII Division"	NIL
" "	3/10/17	6 p.m.	Received A.D.M.S. order No. 74/13/0 dated 3/10/17. Capt CLARKE R.A.M.C. proceeded to WORMHOUDT with A Coast Moto Ambulance to report to A.D.M.S. 63rd R.N.D. Union instructions from D.D.M.S XVIII Corps for duty. Training of Ambulance CONTINUES. Station Commenced 2-30 a.m. and Completed 6-30 a.m. Departure of train from TINGUES for HOPOUTRE.	NIL
7.Camp A16, C5-3 G17.11.28	4/10/17	6 p.m.	Arrived at HOPOUTRE 1-30 a.m. and detrained and marched to 7.Camp A16. C5-3 G17.11.28 arriving there 5-30 a.m. B Section opening a dressing station for admission and inspection of sick.	NIL
" "	5/10/17	6 p.m.	Received medical arrangement A.D.M.S. No. 176/39.D. 6/10/17. Capt Power R. returned from leave in England.	NIL
" "	6/10/17	6 p.m.	Routine Parades.	NIL
" "	7/10/17	6 p.m.	Received A.D.M.S. orders to detail one complete Tent Subdivision to report to A.D.M.S. 11th Division at ESSEX Farm for duty. Received Verbal orders from A.D.M.S. to collect 50 men to proceed to DUHALLOW for duty with 11th Division.	NIL
" "	8/10/17	6 p.m.	3 Other Ranks proceeded to 5th Army Rest Camp. Routine Parades.	NIL

(A7090) Wt. W12859/M1293. 75,000. 1/17. D. D. & L., Ltd. Forms/C.2118/14.

Army Form C. 2118.

WAR DIARY
or
INTELLIGENCE SUMMARY.
(Erase heading not required.)

Instructions regarding War Diaries and Intelligence Summaries are contained in F. S. Regs., Part II. and the Staff Manual respectively. Title pages will be prepared in manuscript.

Place	Date	Hour	Summary of Events and Information	Remarks and references to Appendices
7 Camp A.16.C.6-3 Sheet 28	9/10/17	6 pm	Routine parties: LIEUT. PIERCE detailed for duty as Corps horse Dressing Station vice Capt J.W. CLARKE came to M.D. on 14.8 (A.M.) Field Ambulance	ASCR
"	10/10/17	6pm	Our complete Unit Subaltern returned to H.Q. A/9 of this Ambulance from temporary duty at ESSEX Farm M. Division	RSCR
"	11/10/17	6pm	Capt DOUSE, Renée in charge of working party at DUHALLOW Farm. LIEUT. DOW M.O.R.C. U.S.R. and 4 Other Ranks to 1-9 Corps reinforcement Camp for duty at MERCKEGHEM, Auth Auth N.S. 526/1 D 10/10/17. Six Other Ranks granted leave to England	ASCR
"	12/10/17	6pm	Vaules the forward area with a view to taking over this	ASCR
"	13/10/17	6pm	LIEUT & QM WILLIAMS returned from leave in England. Six Other Ranks granted leave to England	RSCR RSCR
"	14/10/17	6pm	LIEUT DAW R.A.M.C.T.C. returned from leave in England.	RSCR
"	15/10/17	6pm	Routine duties:-	RSCR
"	16/10/17	6pm	Field Ambulance moved to bivouc of Old Corps horse Dressing Station "A.23.C.2.9. Sheet 28 from Camp A.16.C.6.3. map of Sheet 2.8. now opened up C Tent Subdivision for the further of tabled air	RSCR
A.23.C.2.9 Sheet Ref Sheet 28.	17/10/17	6pm	Evacuation and treatment of Venereals	RSCR

WAR DIARY
or
INTELLIGENCE SUMMARY

Army Form C. 2118.

Place	Date	Hour	Summary of Events and Information	Remarks and references to Appendices
A.23.C.2.9. map Ref Sheet 28	18/10/17	6pm	Received 5th Reinforcements from the Base.	RSCR
"	19/10/17	6pm	Received 1st 188th Infy Brigade Operation order No. 148.	RSCR
"	20/10/17	6pm	Two other Ranks granted leave to England: 3 other Ranks to duty from 5th Army reinforcements	RSCR
"	21/10/17	6pm	Commencement of Vaccination; Capt J. MacGregor returned to this Unit for duty from duty with No 2 Canadian C.C.S.	RSCR
"	22/10/17	6pm	Received Notification over A.D.M.S. No. S2.; Attended Conference at 1.S.B. Infy Bongue 2 + 9 am with O.C.'s 18th and Med Officers of Bns. Received Infy Bn'n's Order No. 53.	RSCR
"	23/10/17	6pm	Received A.D.M.S. Operation Order No 54.:- Surg. J.J. KEATLEY. (R.N.) joined this Ambulance for duty and to be taken on the Strength from 22nd inst.	RSCR
C.17.d.2.6 map Ref Sheet 28	24/10/17	6pm	Received 27th Field Ambulance of Division in the line and took over charge of the evacuation of the Forward area.; Relief Completed 6pm.; A.D.O.s of the Ambulance returned to C.17.d.2.6. map Ref Sheet 28.:- No S/3646. Pte WELSH J.G. S/39755. Pte WALSH. M.E. No S/39046. Pte MAWDSLEY L. Killed in Action.	RSCR
"	25/10/17	6pm	Creation of S.A.A. Wounded from Forward area. The number of Stretchers and Blankets taken over from 27th 73rd Amb. Found Great need to reinforce the working of the Forward area.; Sent demands on Corps means Dressing Station urgently. G.S. Wagons refused by O.C. I.M.D.S. without Authority. Sent to 200 Stretchers at first refused to 200 extra Stretchers and Blankets sent Authority granted from Corps: Stretchers and Blankets sent accurately in time for active operations.	R.7.C.R
"	26/10/17	6am	Active Operations Commenced 5:40 am.; Divo Regimental Stretcher bearers of HAWKE Bn reported	

(A7093). Wt. W12859/M1293. 75,000. 1/17. D. D. & L., Ltd. Forms/C.2118/14.

Army Form C. 2118.

WAR DIARY
or
INTELLIGENCE SUMMARY.
(Erase heading not required.)

Instructions regarding War Diaries and Intelligence Summaries are contained in F. S. Regs., Part II. and the Staff Manual respectively. Title pages will be prepared in manuscript.

Place	Date	Hour	Summary of Events and Information	Remarks and references to Appendices
C.19.d.2.6.	26/10/17	6 p.m.	at 7 a.m. at ST JULIEN for duty as Stretcher Bearers.: at 10 a.m. Field Ambulance reported for duty.: Wounded commenced to arrive about 9-30 a.m. A.D.M.S visited A.D.S. ST JULIEN at 10-30 a.m. and remained during active operations. No. 5/20 M Pt. CLASPER.N.J Killed in Action: Bearing Wounded and Stretcher cases coming into A.D.S. in a constant stream all day. Time reports clear of Wounded 6 p.m. Shelling around A.D.S. intense all day.	ack
"	27/10/17	6 p.m.	Recd D.N.V. Ranne detailed from this Ambulance to proceed to 2" R.M.L.I in relief of Surg. Ross (RN) Wounded in action. Capt. Power. MA. Ranne wounded slightly and remained on duty. Received A.D.M.S order No. 55.	ack
"	28/10/17	6 p.m.	O.C 149 (RM) Field Ambulance with one Tent Subdivision arrived 4 p.m in relief of our last Subdivision of this Ambulance.: Relief completed 4 p.m.	ack
A.2.3.c.2.9 start 2.8	29/10/17	6 p.m.	Took over charge of D. Coy Australians from O.C. 149 (RM) Field Ambulance.	ack
"	30/10/17	6 p.m.	Received A.D.M.S Operation order No. 57. Capt Clarke. T. M. Ranne returned from ST JULIEN to HQ of this Field Ambulance at A.2.3. c.2.9.	ack
"	31/10/17	6 p.m.	Received Operation Orders Nos No. 57.	ack

W. R. Renton Lt Col

CONFIDENTIAL.   MEDICAL.

WAR DIARY

of the

148th (Royal Naval) FIELD AMBULANCE.

covering the period

1st November, 1917   to   30th November, 1917.

Lieut.-Col. R.A.M.C.,
Commanding 148th (R.N.) Field Ambulance.

CONFIDENTIAL.   MEDICAL.
....

WAR   DIARY

of the

148th (Royal Naval)   FIELD   AMBULANCE.

covering the period

1st. November, 1917   to   30th. November, 1917.

-:::::::-

Lieut.-Col., R.A.M.C.,
Commanding 148th (R.N.) Field Ambulance.

WAR DIARY
or
INTELLIGENCE SUMMARY.
(Erase heading not required.)

Army Form C. 2118.

Place	Date	Hour	Summary of Events and Information	Remarks and references to Appendices
C.17.d.2.6. Sheet 28	1/11/17	6pm	Took over Command of the forward area from 149 (R.N.) F.A. and relief completed by 4pm.	ACM
"	2/11/17	6pm	No 6/8676 Pte. C. HOPPER of this Ambulance died of wounds - Returned dressing station heavily shelled this of the forward command.	ACM
"	3/11/17	6pm	Capt. J.C. DEUSE R.A.M.C. Struck of the Strength of this unit and proceeded O/O DMS 63rd R.N.D. forward area quiet.	ACM
"	4/11/17	6pm	Lieut. SINCLAIR R.A.M.C. T.C. reported at A/O station for temporary duty from 150th (R.N.) F. Amb. DADMS and OC 1st proceeded F.A. Amb. conducted round the forward area.	ACM
"	5/11/17	6pm	Forward area quiet Returned much shelling.	ACM
"	6/11/17	6pm	S. an. Heavy shelling of St Julien and VAN HEULE and all the roads to the corner of BUFFS Rd. two ammunition lorries struck by a shell and beton fire near A/O station - a Lewis Cycler forced in the middle of the road was blown to pieces by debris and crater for several hours. Owing to heavy shelling with H.E. and Shrapnel found impossible to evacuate cases until this Smoke screen and debris removed and cases piled in. Evacuation commenced 1.15 pm No 5/3618 Sgt J.W. FERGUSON (R.M.) Wounded and sent to Field W.C.S. No 5/3 246. 1/Sgt G.C. TOLSON. Killed in action Received A.D.M.S. Operation order No 58.	ACM
"	7/11/17	6pm	O.C. 1st proceed F.A. Amb. arrived at A.D.S. and at 4pm the personnel of this Ambulance arrived and took over the various posts in relief of this Ambulance in the forward area. Relief completed by 9pm.	ACM
A.23.C.a.9 Sheet 28	8/11/17	6pm	Took over Coys and F.oops from 149 F.A. Amb. Having our unit Subdivision Ambulance in field at Rest Camp L.3. (Sheet 27 D.6) arrived 3pm	ACM

WAR DIARY or INTELLIGENCE SUMMARY

Army Form C. 2118.

Place	Date	Hour	Summary of Events and Information	Remarks and references to Appendices
SCHOOL CAMP L.3. (Sheet 27)	9/11/17	6 pm	Received A.D.M.S. Operation orders No. 59.	R.W.R.
"	10/11/17		2 LIEUT. SINCLAIR Rennie joins this Ambulance from 150 (RN) Fd Amb and struck off the strength of that unit. LIEUT. SINCLAIR Rennie posted to 4" Bedfordshire Regt for temporary duty. Received A.D.M.S. order No 8 26/14. R.	R.W.R.
"	10/11/17	6 pm	Received 189 Inf Bgde order No. 157 and 190 Infantry Bde order No. 132.	R.W.R.
"	11/11/17	6 pm	C Tent Subdivision with Surg. KEATLEY (RN) in command temporarily attached to 190" Infy Brigade. B Tent Subdivision returned from temporary duty at 11th Corps and Fort. R.3.Co. Q (Churk).	R.W.R.
WINNEZEELE J 16.D Sheet 27	12-11-17	1.15 PM	Lieut Col R.T.C. Robertson assumes command of the unit. Capt. T.W. CLARKE RAMC; SR.	Feb
"	"	1.30 PM	The whole Field Amb Less C Tent Subdiv arrived at WINNEZEELE	Feb
"	13-11-17	10.15 AM	Off - WINNEZEELE by march route with 188 Inf Brigade	Feb
LEDRINGHEM C 26 & 8.1 Sheet 27	13-11-17	2 PM	The whole Field Amb Less C Tent Subdiv arrived at LEDRINGHEM.	Feb
"	14-11-17	6 PM	Field and silts found in very dirty condition. No accommodation for sick and silt available for Field Ambulance. Made application to Bnpde & ama commandant for more suitable accommodation. Fatigue parties occupied in cleaning sheds & enumerating of sheets.	Feb

Army Form C. 2118.

WAR DIARY
or
INTELLIGENCE SUMMARY.
(Erase heading not required.)

Instructions regarding War Diaries and Intelligence Summaries are contained in F. S. Regs., Part II. and the Staff Manual respectively. Title pages will be prepared in manuscript.

Place	Date	Hour	Summary of Events and Information	Remarks and references to Appendices
LEDRINGHEM C.27.a.7.6 Sheet 27.	15-11-17	2-30PM	Site occupied by 2nd Training found most suitable for Personnel at C.27.a.7.6. Sheet 27. Tents and moved to this area by Brigade orders. Found accommodation for sick in this area.	Nil.
"	"	"	No 5/18241 Pte. A. BARKER joined for duty from No 2 Coy Div Train	Nil
"	"	"	Surgeon KEATLEY Sub Lt. ANSEN Battalion for duty vice Lieut. H.F. POWELL R.A.M.C. from ANSEN to 148 (R.N.) Field Ambulance for duty.	Nil.
"	16-11-17	3PM.	The undermentioned reinforcements joined for duty from Cyclists Base Depot ROUEN.	Nil.
"	"	"	No 5/3526 Capt. T. ELTRINGHAM. No 5/3179 A/Cpl. C. SIMPSON. No 5/3232 L/Cpl E.G. GREENWOOD	Nil
"	"	"	No S/4313 Pte. S. SHAW. No S/4307 Pte W. POGSON. No S/4121 Pte. P. TATTERSALL	Nil.
"	"	"	No S/4220 Pte. F. WILD. No S/3170 Pte. H. COLLIER. No S/3136 Pte. J. WEBB.	Nil
"	"	"	No S/4327 Pte. T.W. WEAVER. No S/3383 Pte. W.H. LEA. No 35/79 Pte. H.T. BUTTERWORTH.	Nil.
"	"	4PM	No 3077 Sjt. C. BROOKE promoted to Staff Sjt.	Nil
"	"	"	No 35/38 A/Cpl W. TITLEY " " Sergeant.	Nil
"	17-11-17	"	No 1852 Pte. C.E. BARKER returned from leave to ENGLAND	Nil
"	18-11-17	9AM	The following men awarded Decorations as specified	Nil
"	"	"	No S/3538 Sjt. W. TITLEY Bar to Military Medal. S/3527 Pte R. EMMERSON Military Medal	Nil.
"	"	"	No S/3992 Pte. S. CLARK, Military medal. No S/3646 Pte. M. ROBSON Military Medal.	Nil.
"	"	"	No S/3414 Pte. J. Vickers Military Medal. No S/3687 Pte. J. E. RAMSBOTTOM Military Medal.	Nil
"	"	"	No S/3036 A/Sjt J. HOLMES. Military Medal. M2/148629 Pte. L.H. PRICE Military Medal	Nil
"	19-11-17	9AM	No S/2735 Pte. A ROWLAND. No S/2385 Pte. W.H. LEA to 2nd Batt. RMLI for Duty	Nil
"	"	"	No 3/3705 Pte J. FORD returned to duty from 2nd Corps Rest Station.	Nil
"	"	"	Capt. J. McGREGOR returned from leave to PARIS.	Nil.

Army Form C. 2118.

WAR DIARY
or
INTELLIGENCE SUMMARY.
(Erase heading not required.)

Place	Date	Hour	Summary of Events and Information	Remarks and references to Appendices
LEDRINGHEM C27 a7.6	20-11-17	6PM	Collection & inventory of sick } Routine parades & fatigues.	Feb.
	21-11-17	"		Feb.
	22-11-17	"		Feb.
	23-11-17	"		Feb.
"	24-11-17	9AM	S/3203 Capt G.H. SMITH returned from leave to England.	Feb.
"	25-11-17	6PM	Collection & inventory of sick. Routine parades & fatigues.	Feb.
"	26-11-17	11-15	GOC 63 RN Div inspected horse transport	Feb.
"	27-11-17	9PM	Lieut.Col R.T.C. ROBERTSON RAMC awarded D.S.O. Chief Ind Sol Dinner made Commander of Lieut H.B. POWELL injured. Pas ambulance APMS an O.C. Sn 60.	Feb.
"	28-11-17	6.30AM	No S/3694 Pte A.W. THORPE proceeded to England to undergo training for a commission	Feb.
D24 & 9.7 Sheet 27	"	3PM	Inspected moved to D24 & 9.7 sheet 27. HOUTKIRQUE AREA. under 190 Infantry Brigade orders No. 133	Feb.
"	"	"	Capt J. McGREGOR RAMC awarded military cross	Feb.
"	"	6 PM	Lt Col R.T.C ROBERTSON RAMC returned from leave to ENGLAND	Feb.
"	29-11-17	6pm	Routine parades.	Feb.
"	30-11-17	6pm	Capt M.A. POWER RAMC awarded the Military Cross: Lieut. Dow. M.O.R.C. USA and four other ranks reported from 19 Corps Reinforcement Camps.	over

[signature]

CONFIDENTIAL. MEDICAL.

WAR DIARY

of the

148th. (Royal Naval) Field Ambulance

for the period

1st. December, 1917 to 31st. December, 1917.

-:-

COMMITTEE FOR THE MEDICAL HISTORY OF THE WAR
Date -1 FEB. 1918

148TH
(ROYAL NAVAL)
FIELD AMBULANCE.
No..........
Date.. 1.1.18

Lieut.-Col. R.A.M.C.,
Commanding 148th (R.N.) Field Ambulance.

WAR DIARY or INTELLIGENCE SUMMARY

Army Form C. 2118.

Place	Date	Hour	Summary of Events and Information	Remarks and references to Appendices
Dar & 27 Sheet 27	1/12/17	6pm	Lieut. POWELL R.A.M.C.T.F. Posted to 4th Bn Bedford Regt for temporary duty vice Lieut. SINCLAIR R.A.M.C.T.F. to England 1/12/17. Routine parades —	nil
"	2/12/17	6pm	Sunday. N.C.O and 6 men "I.S.D" (R.N) Base Draft rejoined their Unit. Routine parades — Received A.D.M.S order No. 23/27/17	nil
"	3/12/17	6pm	Lieut. D.O.W. McR. USA Smith OJ the Thing to of this Unit on posting to NELSON. Bn for duty	nil
"	4/12/17	8pm	No 23618 Sgt J.W. FERGUSON (R.N) awarded the military medal. Routine parades —	nil
"	5/12/17	6pm	Received A.D.M.S order No. 61 anto 5/12/17. Received 190 "Base movement order. No. Bu 3787/a dates 3/12/17. Lieut DONALDSON R.A.M.C 200 to this Ambulance for duty on taking on strength	nil
7.27C Sheet 27	6/12/17	6pm	ADM this Ambulance 12 noon. Lieut DONALDSON R.A.M.C detailed temporary duty with 4th Bn BEDFORD Regt vice Lieut POWELL R.A.M.C to R.S (sick). (Received 63 Bn administration instruction No. 3,35,4,23,3/a g 5/12/17.	M.C.R.
"	7/12/17	8pm	7/114159 T.S.S.M. (T/W.O Class 1) GREGGAINS. J.M. promoted to rank of Staff Sgt major "W.O Class 1" from 5/3/17 authority A.S.C orders No 106. dated 17/1/17. Received 159 Bn. Bds order No 159. dated 6/12/17.	nil
"	8/12/17	6pm	Received Annual 7 KS. 9th Bass order No 159	nil
"	9/12/17	6pm	Routine parades — previous to PESELHOEK for entraining.	nil

Army Form C. 2118.

WAR DIARY
or
INTELLIGENCE SUMMARY.
(Erase heading not required.)

Instructions regarding War Diaries and Intelligence Summaries are contained in F. S. Regs., Part II. and the Staff Manual respectively. Title pages will be prepared in manuscript.

Place	Date	Hour	Summary of Events and Information	Remarks references to Appendices
LE TRANSLOY CAMP	10/12/17	6 pm	Entraining of Field Ambulance completed by 6.15 am and returned to LE TRANSLOY CAMP, 9pm and arrived LE TRANSLOY CAMP 9pm	nil
"	11/12/17 6pm		Reinforcements (OR) arrived and taken on the strength - One the Rank joined from England.	nil
"	12/12/17 6pm		Routine	nil
"	13/12/17 6pm		Received A/Q M.S. Junction order N° 63. D. 13/12/17. Also 188 Infy Bde order N° 160. A. 13/12/17.	nil
ROCQUIGNY	14/12/17 6pm		Field Amb. moved to ETRICOURT with 188 Infy Brigade and billeted at ROCQUIGNY. One Officer joined this unit from 130 (RN) Field Amb.	nil
MANANCOURT	15/12/17 6pm		Field Amb. arrived with 188 Infy Brigade and billeted at MANANCOURT. 1st Lieut E.L. GOKEY, M.O.R.C. U.S.A. and 1st Lieut R.E. COSTANZO, M.R.C. U.S.A. joined & taken on the strength from 14/12/17. One O Rank reinforcement posted to this Unit. - Received A/Q M.S. of Knot Dn Order N° 64. D. 15/12/17	nil
BARASTRE	16/12/17 7pm		Both Sub Field Amb Sect at O.S. Shut S.J.C. from N° 6 to Cant 2 Div Received 63rd Fd Re received men & encampments N° 176/23. D. 15/12/17	nil
"	17/12/17 6pm		Routine parades and fatigues	nil

Army Form C. 2118.

WAR DIARY
or
INTELLIGENCE SUMMARY.
(Erase heading not required.)

Instructions regarding War Diaries and Intelligence Summaries are contained in F.S. Regs., Part II. and the Staff Manual respectively. Title pages will be prepared in manuscript.

Place	Date	Hour	Summary of Events and Information	Remarks and references to Appendices
BARASTRE	18/11/17	6 pm	Routine parades & fatigues. On the bank reported from No. 2 Corps Rest station.	A.C.R.
"	19/11/17	6 pm	Lieut. J. DONALDSON R.A.M.C. Att'd struck off the strength of this Unit from 6/11/17 on being posted for duty to the Bulford Rd.	A.C.R.
"	20/11/17	6 pm	The following promotions and appointments have been approved with effect from 5/11/17; S/3372 Sgt. TAMBERLAIN. G. to Staff Sgt. General duties. S/3051 Cpl. HINEY. J.A. to 1/Sgt. General duty. No. 6/3676 Pte. S.R. GEAD. Granted Special leave to England as a candidate for No. immediate Plague and Commission. – S/3297 Sgt. BLAND.W.G. joined this unit as a reinforcement.	A.C.R.
"	21/11/17	6 pm	S/3372 Sgt. TAMBERLAIN. G. mentioned in Despatches of the Field Marshal in C. D. 4/11/17.	A.C.R.
"	22/11/17	6 pm	S/3464 Pte. DOUGHTY. W. posted to 1st R.W.L. for duty. – Lieut. COSTANZO. M.O. R.C. V.S.A. proceeded to 63 R.N.D. Wing 5 Corps Reinforcement Camp for temporary duty.	A.C.R.
"	23/11/17	6 pm	S/3982 Pte. GWYTHER. J.W. posted to 247 Field Coy R.E. for duty; No. S/3304 Staff Sgt. N. ELLIOTT. No. S/3203 Cpl. G.H. SMITH. No. S/3539 & L/Cpl. ATTLEY No. S/3638 Pte. T. PASCOE. wounded by enemy bomb	A.C.R.

Army Form C. 2118.

WAR DIARY
or
INTELLIGENCE SUMMARY.
(Erase heading not required.)

Instructions regarding War Diaries and Intelligence Summaries are contained in F. S. Regs., Part II. and the Staff Manual respectively. Title pages will be prepared in manuscript.

Place	Date	Hour	Summary of Events and Information	Remarks and references to Appendices
BARASTRE	24/11/17	6pm	Routine	ACR
"	25/11/17	6pm	Routine	ACR
"	26/11/17	6pm	Routine	ACR
"	27/11/17	6pm	Routine. Received A.D.M.S. order No 67.	ACR
"	28/11/17	6pm	Routine	ACR
"	29/11/17	6pm	Two A.C.O's and 48 nurses attached to 7/60 (RA) 7th Bn. for duty in the forward area. Capt. J. MacGREGOR, M.C. Rome Granted 14 days contact leave to England.	ACR
"	30/11/17	6pm	1st Lieut. GOKEY, M.O.R.C. U.S.A. attached to 5th Corps MDS for temporary duty.	ACR
"	31/11/17	6pm	Eight other ranks granted 14 days leave to England. Received A.D.M.S. order No 74/9/10. Two A.C.O's and 36 nurses returned to A.D.S. for duty in the forward area.	ACR

A.R.Tennant

CONFIDENTIAL. MEDICAL.

WAR DIARY
of the
148th (Royal Naval) Field Ambulance.
for the period,
1st. January 1918 to 31st January 1918.

Lieut.-Col. R.A.M.C.,
Commanding 148th (R.N.) Field Ambulance.

Army Form C. 2118.

WAR DIARY
or
INTELLIGENCE SUMMARY.
(Erase heading not required.)

Instructions regarding War Diaries and Intelligence Summaries are contained in F.S. Regs., Part II. and the Staff Manual respectively. Title pages will be prepared in manuscript.

Place	Date	Hour	Summary of Events and Information	Remarks and references to Appendices
BARASTRE	1/1/18	6 p.m.	Routine	nil
"	2/1/18	6 p.m.	Five O. Ranks granted 14 days leave to England.	nil
"	3/1/18	6 p.m.	Routine	nil
"	4/1/18	10 p.m.	20 O.Ranks rejoined from attached duty with 150 F.A. in France and	nil
"	5/1/18	6 p.m.	No. S/3372 Staff S/S. F. CHAMBERLAIN is appointed acting Staff S/St F.D. from 5/1/18. Auth. A.D.M.S. 55/59 dated 3.1.18. Medical arrangements H.Q.T.M.S. 63. R.W.D. 126/195 dated 4/1/18 received	M.R.
"	6/1/18	6 p.m.	Routine	nil
"	7/1/18	6 p.m.	4 other Ranks granted leave to England	nil
"	8/1/18	6 p.m.	Routine	nil
"	9/1/18	6 p.m.	No. S/3344 Pte TASWELL. I.S.R. awarded 28 days Field Punishment Nº 1. No. S/3545. Pte BLACK. I.H. awarded 14 days F.O. Punishment Nº 1.	nil
"	10/1/18	6 p.m.	One other Rank rejoined this Ambulance from sick leave during	nil
"	11/1/18	6 p.m.	One other Rank granted 14 days leave to England	nil
"	12/1/18	6 p.m.	Capt. H.E. COLYER. R.A.M.C. T.C. posted to this Unit for duty and taken on the Strength	nil

Army Form C. 2118.

WAR DIARY
or
INTELLIGENCE SUMMARY.
(Erase heading not required.)

Instructions regarding War Diaries and Intelligence Summaries are contained in F. S. Regs., Part II. and the Staff Manual respectively. Title pages will be prepared in manuscript.

Place	Date	Hour	Summary of Events and Information	Remarks and references to Appendices
BARASTRE	13/1/18	6pm	1st Lieut GOKEY. M.O.R.C.U.S. rejoined this Ambulance from Meachs duty. 5 Other Ranks M.D. Station. 5 Other Ranks proceeded to 48th C.C.S for temporary duty. Authority A.D.M.S. N.C. 76/6/S.A. 13/1/18. 14 Reinforcements reported and taken on the Strength of this Ambulance.	ACMR
"	14/1/18	6pm	1 Other Ranks granted leave to England. 1 Other Rank rejoined from C.C.S and taken on the strength.	ACMR
"	15/1/18	6pm	Capt James MacGREGOR. M.D. M.C. rejoined from leave to England.	ACMR
"	16/1/18	6pm	Marcel Band arrived at this 1st Ambulance for Inspection of proceeded Pd. 14/1/18. No 53 Mobile Veterinary Section in accordance with A.D.M.S orders No 70/153 Pd. 14/1/18. Capt. COLYER. R.A.M.C. T.C. posted A.H.O.D B. for temporary duty. 1st Lieut GOKEY posted to 150th R.N. L. Amt for temporary duty. 1 Other Ranks reported from leave to England. 5 Other Ranks returned from leave to England.	ACMR ACMR
"	17/1/18	6pm	One Other Rank A.Thedrid (Surd.) admitted with 2 Qrs of this Ambulance according to A.D.M.S order No. 70/153 to receipts men fit. the 53rd Mobile Vet Section.	ACMR ACMR
"	18/1/18	6pm	3 Other Ranks returned from leave to England. 1 Other Rank returned from leave	ACMR ACMR

WAR DIARY
or
INTELLIGENCE SUMMARY.

Army Form C. 2118.

Place	Date	Hour	Summary of Events and Information	Remarks and references to Appendices
BARASTRE	20/1/18	6pm	Received R.O. No. S. O'Envelon Order No. 72. 1st Lieut. GOKEY MORE. V.S. to Shuck off the Strength of this Ambulance and posted to "Y" B- for pieties as medical officer in charge.	nil
"	21/1/18	6pm	One Other Rank returned from leave. Received H.O.S. Order No. 3 5/406/A.7. 5 Other ranks granted leave to England.	nil
"	22/1/18	6pm	Capt. J. MacGREGOR R.K.M.C. proceeded to England on 109/245 and is Struck off the Strength of this unit.	nil
"	23/1/18	6pm	Capt. POWER R.A.M.C. proceeded to 3rd Army School of Sanitation with Return S. 63.2 No. 144/127/4. a. 20/1/18.	nil
"	24/1/18	6pm	Three Other Ranks returned from leave to England.	nil
"	25/1/18	6pm	T/Surg. R.K.SHAW. (R.N.) to return on the Strength of this Unit and posted to 76-149 "RN". 1 O.R. Admitted for temporary duty. 5 Other Ranks returned from leave to England.	nil
"	26/1/18	6pm	Routine	nil
"	27/1/18	6pm	Capt. T.W. CLARKE. M.C. R.A.M.C. and 5 Other Ranks granted 14 days leave to England	nil

Army Form C. 2118.

WAR DIARY
or
INTELLIGENCE SUMMARY.
(Erase heading not required.)

Instructions regarding War Diaries and Intelligence Summaries are contained in F. S. Regs., Part II. and the Staff Manual respectively. Title pages will be prepared in manuscript.

Place	Date	Hour	Summary of Events and Information	Remarks and references to Appendices
BARASTRE	29/1/18	8pm	Routine.	RCW
"	29/1/18	10pm	Lieut & Qrm C.L. WILLIAMS goes on two months leave to England. 30/1/18 to 1/3/18.	RCW
"	30/1/18	6pm	T/S-Sergt H.C. BROADHURST (R.N.) posted to this Unit and is taken on the strength. Lieut H. F. POWELL R.A.M.C. T.C. is struck off the strength of this Unit (auth) A/orrs No 109/249. A. 30/1/18.	RCW
"	31/1/18	6.6pm	Capt A.G. WILKINSON. R.Amme.T.C. is attached for temporary duty to the Unit From 149 (RN) F. Amb	RCW

[signature]
LIEUT.-COLONEL, R.A.M.C.
COMMANDING 1st (N.M.) FIELD AMBULANCE

No. 146. T.C.

COMMITTEE FOR THE
MEDICAL HISTORY OF THE WAR
Date −8 APR. 1918

CONFIDENTIAL.
....

WAR DIARY.

of

148th. (Royal Naval) FIELD AMBULANCE.

From   1st. February 1918.

To   28th. February 1918.

Lieut. Colonel R.A.M.C.,
Commanding 148th. (R.N.) FIELD AMBULANCE.

Army Form C. 2118.

WAR DIARY
or
INTELLIGENCE SUMMARY.

(Erase heading not required.)

Instructions regarding War Diaries and Intelligence Summaries are contained in F. S. Regs., Part II. and the Staff Manual respectively. Title pages will be prepared in manuscript.

Place	Date	Hour	Summary of Events and Information	Remarks and references to Appendices
BARASTRE	1/2/18	6pm	No 5/43 RG Pte MORTIMER. H. proceeded to No 2 (G) Div Train for temporary duty. 9 other ranks returned from leave to England.	nil
"	2/2/18	6pm	Routine	nil
"	3/2/18	6pm	11 other ranks granted leave to England. Capt WILKINSON. R.A.M.C. T.F. proceeded to 33rd Sanitary Section to assume temporary charge	nil
"	4/2/18	6pm	No 5/33 OTC Staff Sgt ELLIOTT. N. promoted to W.O. class II on appointment as Q-M Sgt of 146 (R.N) Field Ambulance	nil
"	5/2/18	6pm	Two reinforcements posted to the Unit - for duty and taken on the Strength. Capt TIMMS. C.J. Rennie posted to the Ambulance for duty and is taken on the Strength. No 5/3496 Cpl BATE. G. awarded Decoration MILITAIRE (Auth) R.D. No 3665 dated 2-2-23 M.G.C.O.Y.	nil
"	6/2/18	6pm	No 5/3344 Pte HASWELL. I.	nil
"	7/2/18	6pm	6 other ranks returned from leave to England.	nil
"	8/2/18	6pm	9 other ranks granted leave to England. Lieut Col BROADHURST (RN) returned from Course of instruction of Army School of Sanitation. Orders 3 clearly received at Divisional ambulance and divisional Rest Station	nil

Army Form C. 2118.

WAR DIARY
or
INTELLIGENCE SUMMARY.
(Erase heading not required.)

Instructions regarding War Diaries and Intelligence Summaries are contained in F.S. Regs., Part II. and the Staff Manual respectively. Title pages will be prepared in manuscript.

Place	Date	Hour	Summary of Events and Information	Remarks and references to Appendices
BAPAUME	10/1/18	6 p.m.	Routine	
"	11/1/18	6 p.m.	Received A.D.M.S operation order No. 43. Received transport appreciation from A.D.M.S	A.W.
"	12/1/18	6 p.m.	A.D.M.S inspection. Issued transport instruction. 14th Field Transport inspected by No. 63 Sup. Train.	A.W.
"			Routine :- Visit HQ. of 7 S.B. and 59 Field Ambulance at METZ preparatory to taking over charge of the forward area.	Reed
"	13/1/18	6 p.m.	Relief this day of 4th Canadian Casualty Clearing Station by 6 mm. D.D.M.S. Corps inspected divisional Rel. Station. Ambulance completely taken over and divisional Rel. Station by No. 150 R.M.Field Ambulance and	A.W.
"	14/1/18	6 p.m.	completed by 10 a.m.	
METZ (A.B.C.&P. Sheet 57.C.)			HQ & B. & C. of the Ambulance moved to METZ. Q.70. Co. 9. Sheet 57.C.b.) Took over HQ & A. of 7 S.B. Field Ambulance. Adv. of A. working formed collecting post at TRESCAULT Q.10.a.4.5 and the advanced working to tip & Ranving completed by 10 a.m.	
"			Relief of forward posts and advanced dressing station on Right Bk. completed by 6.P.M.	
"			Capt. T. W. CLARKE NZ. R.M.C. returned from Leave in England. The following Instructions and of of instrument were approved with effect from 10/1/18. No. 5/3397. A/sergt. Sgt. CHAMBERLAIN.G. to Staff Sgt. G. Duties. No. 5/3538. Sgt. TITLEY. W.B. a/Staff Sgt. G. Duties.	A.W. / Reed
"	15/1/18	6 p.m.	Routine. 63 R.M. Division medical arrangements No. 146/10.	A.W. / Reed
"	16/1/18	6 p.m.	Surg. Bearce-GOULD (R.N) and Surg. SHAW (R.N) joined this unit for duty from 149 F.A. Amb.	Reed
"	17/1/18	6 p.m.	2. Other Ranks rejoined from 150 (R.N) F.A. Amb.	A.W.
"	18/1/18	6 p.m.	17 Other Ranks returned 14 days leave to England; two Other Ranks rejoined from 150 F.A. Amb.	A.W.

WAR DIARY or INTELLIGENCE SUMMARY

Army Form C. 2118.

Place	Date	Hour	Summary of Events and Information	Remarks and references to Appendices
METZ (2 W.Co.A)	19/4/18	6 p.m.	Received 63"(RN) Division record book over Yr.	nil
"	20/4/18	6 p.m.	Surg. Rear Gould proceeded to 2" RMLI for temporary duty for 12 hours. D/W Ramc; Lieut Khan Ramc returned from leave to England.	nil
"	21/4/18	12 p.m.	Capt H.C. COLYER Ramc TC posted to 2nd RMLI and is struck off the strength of this unit from this instant. N° DM 2/0/2694/1. Pte HINCLIFFE A. Its e MT found this unit for duty from the 63rd DSC It also have returned from leave to England	nil
			Handed over the records of the Armoured Right sector to the N° 6 52 Aml 2" Division Relief completed by 6 p.m.	nil
"	22/4/18	6 p.m.	10 other ranks granted 14 days leave to England	nil
"	23/4/18	6 p.m.	Took over the forwarding posts from O.C. 6 London F° Aml (2) Division in the Fimelica Sector (K.2.8.a.2.1) – Bearer Relay posts at L.25 b.1.5. and K.20 a.2.8. Car posts L.26.a.9.1 Relief completed by 6 p.m.	nil
"	24/4/18	6 p.m.	5. Reinforcements joined this unit and are taken on the strength: some transport moved to ROCHELLE P°5. Central, minus 3 setting P.Q 2 6.E.P. Capt. TIMMS MC Ramc posted to 4" Bedford Rgt. for temporary duty 2 other Ramc & medical Personnel of Howe Bn posted to this unit and taken on the strength. One other Ramc returned from leave to England	nil
"	25/4/18	6 p.m.	Particulars of Personnel from Particulars of Armoured areas	nil
"	26/4/18	6 p.m.	T/Surg H.C. BROADHURST posted to 2nd Bn RMLI; T/Surg R.K SNAW (RN) posted to Drake Bn; T/Surg A.L. PEARCE-GOULD posted to 2/2 Bn RMLI. Capt H.C COLYER Ramc, T.C. posted to Base Deport from leave to England	nil

WAR DIARY
or
INTELLIGENCE SUMMARY.

Army Form C. 2118.

Place	Date	Hour	Summary of Events and Information	Remarks and references to Appendices
METZ (A.o.C.6.9.) Sheet 57.	25/2/18	6pm	Lieut. H. DAW. R.A.M.C. posted to this unit from 2nd Bn R.M.L.I. Lieut. A.J. GORDON. M.O.R.N.V.R. attached to the unit from 150th (R.N.) F.A. The remnants of this unit moved from LECHELLE to RUYAULCOURT (P.10.C.) Sheet 57C.	[initials]

[Signature] Lieut.-Colonel, R.A.M.C.
COMMANDING 148 (R.N.) FIELD AMBULANCE

148TH
(ROYAL NAVAL)
FIELD AMBULANCE.
No. _____
Date 25.2.18

160/2849.

COMMITTEE FOR THE
HISTORICAL HISTORY OF THE WAR
12 MAY 1918
Date

148 F.D.

March
10/1/18

Army Form C. 2118.

WAR DIARY
or
INTELLIGENCE SUMMARY.
(Erase heading not required.)

Vol 22

Instructions regarding War Diaries and Intelligence Summaries are contained in F. S. Regs., Part II. and the Staff Manual respectively. Title pages will be prepared in manuscript.

Place	Date	Hour	Summary of Events and Information	Remarks and references to Appendices
METZ Q20.c.6.9	1/3/18	6 pm	5 Other Ranks returned from leave to England	nil
"	2/3/18	6 pm	Lieut. P Qr Williams (R.N) returned from leave to England	nil
"	3/3/18	6 pm	All stretcher cases are newly evacuated from L.31.a.3.9 Chilli SCy returned stretchers to return and conveyed that on cars TOCTMDS by HAVRINCOURT. A steam disinfector for the treatment of scabies & Ahnis and other W.P. TRESCAULT and at A.D.S. HAVRINCOURT for the treatment of scabies Clothing and other W.P. TRESCAULT	nil
"	4/3/18	6 pm	2 N.C.Os and 16 men sent this week as reinforcements — 10 Oth. Ranks granted 14 days leave to England	nil
"	5/3/18	6 pm	Received medical arrangements A.D.M.S 63 WGMD No 823/48/2	nil
"	6/3/18	6 pm	Capt. T.W. CLARKE returned at A.D.S L.31.a.3.9. 2/Lieut DAW Reune — Capt Clarke to W.W.C.P.	nil
"	7/3/18	6 pm	Both over a large dugout at Q14.C.5.6 Sheet 57C from 6 London F. Amb 47 Div	nil
"	8/3/18	6 pm	4 Reinforcements joined from the base and are taken on the strength. 5 Oth Ranks returned from leave to England	nil
"	9/3/18	6 pm	7 Oth Ranks returned from leave to England	nil
"	10/3/18	6 pm	10 Oth Ranks granted 14 days leave to England. Sent Qr. & Field Ambulance train to Q14.C.8.6 Sheet 57C	nil

Army Form C. 2118.

WAR DIARY
or
INTELLIGENCE SUMMARY.
(Erase heading not required.)

Instructions regarding War Diaries and Intelligence Summaries are contained in F. S. Regs., Part II. and the Staff Manual respectively. Title pages will be prepared in manuscript.

Place	Date	Hour	Summary of Events and Information	Remarks and references to Appendices
14 C.C.S.	11/3/18	6pm	The following appointments have been approved 8/3/18. Capt. T.W. CLARKE. M.C. R.A.M.C. to a/major (from M.A. POWER. M.C. R.A.M.C. to a/major) Auth. 63 (RN) Div. Routine Order No. 3815.	rcd
"	12/3/18	6pm	Instrument area heavily shelled with 9H3 (mustard) gas and several cases of gas (mustard) from this unit were evacuated to 48 C.C.S. diagnosed Gas (Shell M). A/major M.A. POWER. M.C. R.A.M.C. 148 (RN) F.Amb. wounded. Superficial shell wd right knee and remaining on duty.	rcd
"	13/3/18	6pm	A/Major McKeehr J. this Unit evacuated to 48 C.C.S. diagnosed Gas Shell W. Capt. A.C. COLYER R.A.M.C. 148 (RN) F.Amb. evacuated to 48 C.C.S. diagnosed Gas (Shell W)	rcd
"	14/3/18	6pm	Received C3 (RN) Div medical arrangement No. 146/27. Gas 73-3-18. a/Capt Robb joined 148 (RN) F.A. temporary and Cmdg. Evacuated Gas Shell W. The under named of 148 (RN) F.A. diagnosed Gas (Shell W) a/Major T.W. CLARKE M.C. R.A.M.C. diagnosed Gas (Shell W) and remaining on duty. Lieut. GORDON MD. R.U.S.A. 2 was attacked 8 ½ for duty with 148 F.A. I.C.M.D. staff. Capt. SCALES R.A.M.C. reported for temp duty from 150 (RN) F. Amb. Received C3 (RN) Div Medical arrangements No. 23/33 d. 14/3/18.	rcd
"	15/3/18	6pm	Sgts. Rew no evacuated to C.C.S. diagnosed Gas (Shell M). Capt. ILEO and Capt WILKINSON R.A.M.C. evacuated to base for temporary duty. 3.D bearers relieved of this Unit for tempy duty. Permits London T/A 47 Div. 149 (RN) F. Amb. Strength detail 3.O bearer. Lieut D+W RANE. 148 (RN) F.A. temporary to a/Capt M.O.S. diagnosed Gas Shell W.	rcd

WAR DIARY
INTELLIGENCE SUMMARY

Army Form C. 2118.

Place	Date	Hour	Summary of Events and Information	Remarks and references to Appendices
Q14.C.6.8.	16/3/18	6pm	Lt.Col. R.T.C. ROBERTSON D.S.O. assumed command (Shell W) and 150 7.M. W/Head Station & other Ranks of this unit evacuated to C.C.S. gassed or shelled (W). Lieut. R.F. COSTANZO W.S.M.O.R.C. reformed from 63" (RN) Div Wing S Corps Reinforcement Camp	nil
"	17/3/18	6pm	Capt. C.G. TIMMS M.C. R.A.M.C. rejoins the Unit for temporary duty vice Lt Bedford	nil nil
"	18/3/18	6pm	Capt. WILKINSON R.A.M.C. 149 (RN) F.A. proceeds R.S.I.M.D.S. for duty. A sewer sub-division of the 4 London Field Ambulance relieves in the forward area, proceed to reform their own unit. 9/47 "evinces Romlin Trench by the forward area	nil nil
"	19/3/18	6pm		nil
"	20/3/18	6pm	H.Q. of Field Ambulance moved to RUYAULCOURT. Our two ambulance cars totally destroyed by shell fire and No. 5/4322 Pte TYSON J. and No. M/703228 Pte DUGDALE.J. Killed	nil
"	21/3/18	6pm		nil
RUYAULCOURT (P.10 Central sheet 57.C)	22/3/18	6pm	Major ANDERSON D.S.O. M.C. R.A.M.C. evac for temporary duty from 150 Front Advanced Dressing Station & Right Sub Sector withdrawn to TRES CAVET (Q10 A.5.4). Walking wounded Collecting post withdrawn to Q9 A.6.4.". H Qrs of unit moved to NEUVILLE (P11 d.2.8)	nil
"	23/3/18	6pm	Advanced Dressing Station was withdrawn to NEUVILLE (P11.d.2) about 2 a.m. I visited 1 S.G. Brussel's Osts at 6 am. H.Qrs of unit moved to BUS (Q23.d.5.4) at 3 am	nil

(Apg94). Wt. W12899/M1293. 73,000. 1/17. D. D. & L., Ltd. Forms/C.2118/14.

WAR DIARY or INTELLIGENCE SUMMARY

Army Form C. 2118.

Place	Date	Hour	Summary of Events and Information	Remarks and references to Appendices
			which was stationed near the A.D.S. NEUVILLE and spoke to the G.O.C. whom I informed of my Medical posts. About 12 noon the A.D.S. was withdrawn to BUS (R.23.c.5.4) and the Q.M. of unit moved to LE TRANSLOY (N.24.d.5.5). I reached H.Q. Brigade A.I.Qn. at 9.30 a.m. and spoke to G.O.1 and Staff Capt. 189 Brigade whom I informed of my medical posts, of the being informed of the new position of the line. From BUS the trains (cars) with wounded were taken away to a forward of the trenches East-Station. Cars were evacuated by Motor Ambulance. The A.D.S. remained at BUS for the whole day. Nr. 23° and early morning of the 24°. Most BUS was evacuated by the enemy in the morning of 24°. About 4·30 am I visited 189 and 190 Infantry H.Q. & H.Q. 26 ROCQUIGNY and had an interview with both G.O.C's regarding the tactical situation, and I informed them of my medical posts.	A.R.R.
LE TRANSLOY (N.24.d.5.5) FRICOURT	24/3/18	6 p.m.	Advanced Dressing Station was withdrawn about 7 am from BUS to LE TRANSLOY. H.Qn. of unit moved to LES BOEUFS (T.4 cent.) and from there to BEZANTIN LE GRAND (S.15.a.2.8). A.D.S. withdrawn from LE TRANSLOY to LES BOEUFS and from there to BEZANTIN LE GRAND. These medical posts were mobile and were frequently moved owing to the tactical situation and the rapid advance of the enemy. Severely wounded personnel of this unit are men's H.Qn. of this unit moved to FRICOURT from the A.D.S. LES BOEUF.	A.R.R.
BOUZINCOURT (W.X.C.6.5) 57 D	25/3/18	6 p.m.	Field Ambulance H.Qr. moved at 1 am to 1/2 mile on MILLENCOURT-ALBERT Rd (E.1.6.5.8. Sys.D.) an Advanced Dressing Station was established at POZIERES (X.4.C.0.6) and a contact at (W.24.C.D.4). H.Qr. & Field Ambulance moved to BOUZINCOURT. A.D.S. withdrawn from	

WAR DIARY or INTELLIGENCE SUMMARY

Army Form C. 2118.

Place	Date	Hour	Summary of Events and Information	Remarks and references to Appendices
BOIZINCOURT	25/8/16	6pm	POZIERES and a Mobile A.D.S. formed at THIEPVAL. Q.4.A.2.4 under command of Capt. TIMMS. At 6pm H.Qrs of Field Amb. moved to LEAVILLERS. (O.23.b. & 57.57D) Major T.W. CLARKE handed the F.A. from 149 R.M.F.Amb.	ACK
LEAVILLERS (O.23.a.5.7) 57	26/8/16	6pm	An Advanced Dressing Station was established at HEDAUVILLE (P.34.D.2.2) and a Car post at MARTINSART (W.3.a.4.4) and an Advanced Medical Officer, personnel and Cars at MES M.L. Rly Station (Q.28.c.3.6). Commencement of relay in the Forward area by Field Amb of 112 Div.	ACK
"	27/8/16	6pm	Relief of Forward area by 36th/12 Div completed by 4.30 a.m. and advance handed over. Received A.D.M.S order No P.II. instructing the affiliation of this 7 Field to 75/8 Brigade for duty. An A.D.S was established at Q.32.a.5.4. on the MARTINSART-ENGLEBELMER Rd for a temporary duty. Lt Major POWER M.M.C. Major Anderson and Capt Scott rejoined 15/37F and Major POWER rejoined this Unit from 15/37F. Lieut WALKER and MORRIS M.O.R.C. U.S.A. reported for temporary duty from 14.9.7F.	ACK
"	28/8/16	6pm	Lieut MORRIS transfer R.M.N.I. for duty. Lt Col ROBERTSON R.A.M.C returned to Dept from 15/37F and in consequence the A.D.S. withdrawn 158 Inf Brigade released in the Forward Area and motor cyclist from this unit attached to 75/8 Brigade H.Q. Received A.D.M.S order No 7/90. Cases to be evacuated by a Fd Amb of the 12 Div at the nearing Station at 0.30 in F.A.	ACK
"	29/8/16	6pm	Lieut WALKER and Lieut STEFFEN. M.O.R.C. U.S.A are posted to this Unit and are taken on the Strength	ACK

Army Form C. 2118.

WAR DIARY
or
INTELLIGENCE SUMMARY.
(Erase heading not required.)

Instructions regarding War Diaries and Intelligence Summaries are contained in F. S. Regs., Part II. and the Staff Manual respectively. Title pages will be prepared in manuscript.

Place	Date	Hour	Summary of Events and Information	Remarks and references to Appendices
LEALVILLERS (O.23.b.5.7) (Sheet 57b)	30/3/16	6pm	Collector and Evacuator of sick from 168 Brigade, I wanted 168 Brigade HQ re also all Bn HdQrs and Bn medical offices.	MR
"	31/3/16	6pm	Capt. Howell Gwynne JONES, RAMC. SR. to posted to the Unit and to taken on the strength. Collector Evacuator of sick from 168 Inf. Brigade.	MR

(signature)
LIEUT.-COLONEL, R.A.M.C.
COMMANDING (1/4 R.N.) FIELD AMBULANCE.

160/2900.

148th Field Ambulance.

Dec 1918.

CONFIDENTIAL. **148TH (ROYAL NAVAL) FIELD AMBULANCE.** MEDICAL.

No. ....
Date. 1/5/18.

WAR DIARY

of the

148th (Royal Naval) Field Ambulance

for the period

1st April, 1918 to 30th April, 1918.

In the Field,
1:5:18.

Lieut.-Col. R.A.M.C.,
Commanding 148th (R.N.) Field Ambulance.

Army Form C. 2118.

WAR DIARY
or
INTELLIGENCE SUMMARY.
(Erase heading not required.)

Vol 23

Instructions regarding War Diaries and Intelligence Summaries are contained in F. S. Regs., Part II. and the Staff Manual respectively. Title pages will be prepared in manuscript.

Place	Date	Hour	Summary of Events and Information	Remarks and references to Appendices
LEALVILLERS O.23 b 5.7 Sheet 57D	1/4/18	6 pm	5 other ranks returned from leave to England	nil
"	2/4/18	6 pm	4 other ranks " "	nil
"	3/4/18	6 pm	Received R.D.'s orders to proceed to CLAIRFAYE and take over Aerodrome	nil
CLAIRFAYE (O.29.6.9 Sheet 57D)	4/4/18	10 am	Ambulance moved to CLAIRFAYE move completed 9am	nil
"	5/4/18	6 pm	30 aerodrome wick stores over 529/92 A. O/4/18. Two clerks detailed for duty with 36 & 78 Aust.12 Div. Lieut WALKER MRC USA and 2 O.R. were detailed for duty with 36 & 78 Aust.12 Div	nil
"	6/4/18	5 pm	The above transport of this unit moved from PUCHEVILLERS (N.21.6.) to Aerodrome CLAIRFAYE. Lieut CONSTANZO Wr ORC USA detailed for duty with 36/9 Ami 12 Div. Received Orns Order No 76/141. Detail/4/18 to establish a qro bestinent centre at Aerodrome CLAIRFAYE, with Major M.TURNER in Charge. H.Q. 9pm Losses from leave 1.4.18 to 9.P.R. (Di-Chlorphenyl Arsine) 1 Officer 8.P.R. (Di-Chlorphenyl Arsine 9.-)	nil nil
"	7/4/18	6 pm	6 am to 8 pm gassed cases treated	nil
"	8/4/18	8 pm	Sgt Major CRENSHAW. RAMC returned from leave England 6 am to 8 pm 1 Officer and 14/ other ranks treated through gas Antie (mustard gas).	nil
"	9/4/18	8 pm	62 reinforcements received and are taken on the strength. N.B. gassed cases from 2am 8.4.18. - 331 O.R. (mustard gas) except a few officers to base cases	nil
"	10/4/18	8 pm	Lieut WALKER MC USA evacuated to C.C.S. sick	nil

Army Form C.2118.

WAR DIARY
or
INTELLIGENCE SUMMARY.
(Erase heading not required.)

Instructions regarding War Diaries and Intelligence Summaries are contained in F.S. Regs., Part II. and the Staff Manual respectively. Title pages will be prepared in manuscript.

Place	Date	Hour	Summary of Events and Information	Remarks and references to Appendices
CLAIRFAYE (0.29 b.6.9) Sheet 57 D	11/4/18	6pm	Grand Cercle through Gas Cercle from Gas Officer to G Officers & 3 S.B. NCO all mustard Gas for all one case pieces of a few Blue Cross Cases.	nil.
"	12/4/18	6pm	Grand Cercle from 6am to 6pm. 4 Officers & 40 O.R. (Mustard Gas) as per Blue Cross Cases.)	nil.
"	13/4/18	6pm	Rec'd A.D.M.S. order No. 76 dated 13/4/18.	nil.
"	14/4/18	6pm	Handed over working of Corps Gas Centre to No. 53 F. Amb. 1st Div.	nil.
"	14/4/18	6pm	Ambulance marched to PUCHEVILLERS and camped at N.25.a.9.4 Sheet 57.D. arriving at 11pm.	nil.
PUCHEVILLERS N.25.a.9.4. Sheet 57 D	15/4/18	6pm	1 Other Ranks granted Special leave to England. Extracting scale from 15 Gen. H9. Received 158 Inft Brigade nurses for winter in Reserve dated 15/4/17.	nil.
"	16/4/18	6pm	Routine Parades. 14 Other Ranks no Improvement received and one sent to this Ambulance and taken on the strength.	nil.
"	17/4/18	8.30pm	Routine. Review Parade.	nil.
"	18/4/18	8.30pm	Routine. " " Received 5th Gen. S. 6 Div. No. 12 S/30974.	nil.
"	19/4/18	8.30pm	Routine. " "	nil.
"	20/4/18	6pm	Routine. " " Lieut COSTANZO posted R.A.M.D. to DRAKE Bn and Surg C. LEAKE (R.N.) posted to " this week.	nil.
"	21/4/18	8pm	Routine.	nil.
"	22/4/18	8pm	Rec'd R.S. Inft Brigade order B.M. 6 S.D. No. 72/4/15	nil.

Army Form C. 2118.

WAR DIARY
or
INTELLIGENCE SUMMARY.

(Erase heading not required.)

Instructions regarding War Diaries and Intelligence Summaries are contained in F. S. Regs., Part II. and the Staff Manual respectively. Title pages will be prepared in manuscript.

Place	Date	Hour	Summary of Events and Information	Remarks and references to Appendices
PUCHEVILLERS (N 28 a.9.4.) Sheet 57D	23/4/18	6pm	Routine Parades	RCR
"	24/4/18	6pm	Routine Parades.	RCR
"	25/4/18	6pm	Received A.D.M.S. order 123/310 d. 25/4/18.	RCR
"	26/4/18	6pm	The following Other ranks awarded the military medal. - No S/3372 Staff Sergt. TAMBERLIN,G. No S/3971 P/C/R DILLON J. - No 6/4004 Pte. A. DITCH BURN. No S/2300 Pte. J. MILLS No M/2/107129 Pte. G.R. FREER. A.S.C.M.T. Auth 63rd RND Routine orders No 3973 dated 26/4/18	RCR
"	27/4/18	6pm	Eight Reinforcements now posted to this Unit and are taken on the Strength from 27/4/18. Three other Ranks joined the Unit from 178th R.M.L.I. and are taken on the Strength from 26/4/18	RCR
"	28/4/18	6pm	Received A.D.M.S. order No 123/312 dated 28/4/18. Received 188 Inf Brigade order No 3. d. 28/4/18	RCR
"	29/4/18	6pm	Routine Parades.	RCR
"	30/4/18	6pm	In accordance with A.D.M.S 63 R.N.D. order No 123/312 a section of this Unit attended 188 Inf Brigade manoeuvres	RCR

Commanding "?" (R.N.) Field Ambulance

MEDICAL   CONFIDENTIAL.

WAR DIARY

of the

148th (Royal Naval) Field Ambulance

for the period,

1st. May, 1918   to   31st. May, 1918

Lieut.-Col. R.A.M.C.,
Commanding 148th (R.N.) Field Ambulance.

WAR DIARY
or
INTELLIGENCE SUMMARY.

Army Form 2118.

Place	Date	Hour	Summary of Events and Information	Remarks and references to Appendices
PUCHEVILLERS N.24.A.9.4 Sheet 57D	1/5/18	6pm	Routine Parade.	RCR
"	2/5/18	6pm	Routine Parade.	RCR
"	3/5/18	6pm	Routine Parade.	RCR
"	4/5/18	6pm	Temp Captain C.G. TIMMS Rame MC arrived and was to MC dated 3/5/18. Posted to No. 76 F.S.g. Capt TIMMS MC Rame posted to 4th Bn Royal Fusiliers for temporary duty.	RCR
"	5/5/18	6pm	Received 6.5 R.N Medical kit order No. 83.	RCR
"	6/5/18	6pm	Capt TIMMS Rame on posting to 7 Bn R.F. is struck off the strength of this unit from 4/5/18.	RCR
"	7/5/18	6pm	Received 6.3 R.N.D Medical arrangements No. 2 = N° S/3054 Cpl A. O'DELL	RCR
"	8/5/18	6pm	attached to 4 SSD Amb. trans, attached to Transport. moved to Rendezvous CLAIRFAYE.	RCR RSR
CLAIRFAYE D.2.9.6.9	9/5/18	6pm	took over Corps Eye Cadre from 53 & 7 A.T. Ader. Lieut S.M. MORRIS MORC USA posted to this unit and is taken on the strength.	RCR
"	10/5/18	6pm	to care + cases admitted. Routine 14 Eye Cases admitted from 6pm to 10pm.	RCR
"	11/5/18	6pm	3 cases + Eye admitted from 6pm to 10pm. Received MED. Attachment Defence scheme.	RCR
"	12/5/18	6pm	N° S/3447 Pte A. CRIPPEN granted 14 days Special leave to England	RCR

Army Form 2118.

WAR DIARY
or
INTELLIGENCE SUMMARY.
(Erase heading not required.)

Instructions regarding War Diaries and Intelligence Summaries are contained in F.S. Regs., Part II. and the Staff Manual respectively. Title pages will be prepared in manuscript.

Place	Date	Hour	Summary of Events and Information	Remarks and references to Appendices
CLAIRFAYE O.29.c.6.9.	13/5/16	6pm	Nos/3145. Pte S.S. SUTTON. Gen (W) 14 Bays Special leave to England. No 1 Gas case admitted.	Nil
"	14/5/16	6pm	No. S/3992. Pte M. LEVY. joined 1st to 63 RND Signal Coy and is Struck off the Strength of this unit. No 1 Gas case admitted. 2. O'Ranks gone sick to 6pm.	Nil
"	15/5/16	6pm	No 1 Gas case admitted from 6am to 6pm. 1 OR	Nil
"	16/5/16	6pm	No. 9. Gas cases admitted from 6am to 6pm. 1 OR. 1/Lieut STEFFEN. MORCJSF. Posted to 3/1" Bryants R.F. for temporary duty.	Nil
"	17/5/16	6am	No 1 Gas case admitted 6pm to 6pm. G. OR	N.R.R.
"	18/5/16	6pm	No 7 Gas cases admitted 6am to 6pm. 31. OR	N.R.R.
"	19/5/16	6pm	1/Surg (C. LEAKE. RN Posted to 1st Bn RNLI and is Struck off the Strength of this unit from 19/5/16. Capt. H. GWYNNE JONES R.A.M.C.(SR) Posted to 27th M.A.C. and is Struck off the Strength of this unit from 19/5/16. No 7 Gas cases admitted 2 Officers and 12 O.R. Men 6am to 6pm.	Nil
"	20/5/16	6pm	No. 7 Gas cases admitted from 6pm to 6pm. 5 Officers and 21 O.R. 1/Lieut MARR'S. MORCJSA. Posted to 1/13th RNLI. and Struck off the Strength of this unit from 22/5/16.	N.R.R.
"	21/5/16	6pm	Capt EVANS R.A.M.C is taken on the Strength of this unit from 21/5/16 and to Clairfaye attached to 63rd RN Divisional Wing. No 1 Gas case admitted 8 Officers and 266. OR from 6pm to 6pm.	N.R.R.

Army Form C. 2118.

WAR DIARY
or
INTELLIGENCE SUMMARY.
(Erase heading not required.)

Instructions regarding War Diaries and Intelligence Summaries are contained in F. S. Regs., Part II. and the Staff Manual respectively. Title pages will be prepared in manuscript.

Place	Date	Hour	Summary of Events and Information	Remarks and references to Appendices
CLAIRFAYE O29 d 6.9	24/5/18	5pm	I/Corps Commander inspected No 70 Gas Centre.	nil
"	25/5/18	6pm	Gas case admitted from 6pm to 6pm 6 Officers and 19 O.R.	nil
"	26/5/18	6pm	N:S. Gas cases admitted from 6pm to 6pm 1 Officer and 61 O.R.	
"	"	7pm	Lieut V Q= C.L. WILLIAMS. 146 (Rn) T² Amb. murdered in Dispensary CC 2/5/4/18	nil
"	25/5/18	6pm	Gas cases admitted 6pm to 6pm. 1 Officer & 17. O.R.	nil
"	26/5/18	6pm	Gas cases admitted from 6pm to 6pm. 1 Officer & 31. O.R.	nil
"	"	"	" 2. Officers & 12. O.R.	nil
"	27/5/18	6pm	At Lieut. STEFFEN. V.S.M.O.R.C. posted to 317. Brigade R.F.A motor shuttle off. the strength of this unit	nil
"	"	"	Gas cases admitted 4 Officers & 129. O.R.	nil
"	28/5/18	6pm	Gas cases admitted 2 Officers & 115. O.R.	nil
"	29/5/18	6pm	" 2. " v 31. O.R	nil
"	30/5/18	6pm	A/Cpl. R.T.C. ROBERTSON. reassigned in departure YC in C. 25/5/18	nil
"	31/5/18	6pm	Received A.D.M.S. medical unit order N° 6.5 and medical arrangements N° 3. 21 tent/Common posted to this Unit and taken on the strength	nil

(A7092) Wt. W13839/M1293-75,000. 1/17. D. D. & L., Ltd. Forms/C.2118/14.

WAR DIARY
or
INTELLIGENCE SUMMARY

(Erase heading not required.)

Army Form C. 2118.

Place	Date	Hour	Summary of Events and Information	Remarks and references to Appendices
FAIRFAYE O.29 b.6.9.	31/5/18	10pm	1 ac case admitted from Opr 6.6pm, 14 othr Ranks	Rank

Signed,
....
LIEUT.-COLONEL, R.A.M.C.
COMMANDING 148 (H.M.) FIELD AMBULANCE.

MEDICAL.   CONFIDENTIAL.

W A R   D I A R Y

of the

148th (Royal Naval) Field Ambulance

for the period

1st. June, 1918 to 30th June, 1918.

                                            Lieut.-Col. R.A.M.C.,
30th June.1918.   Commanding 148th (R.N.) Field Ambulance.

Army Form C. 2118.

WAR DIARY
or
INTELLIGENCE SUMMARY
(Erase heading not required.)

Instructions regarding War Diaries and Intelligence Summaries are contained in F. S. Regs., Part II. and the Staff Manual respectively. Title pages will be prepared in manuscript.

Place	Date	Hour	Summary of Events and Information	Remarks and references to Appendices
CLARZAYE O.V.A. 6.6.9	1/6/18	6pm	No.5/3151 Staff Sgt. B.J. CARR. promoted to W.O. Class II on appointment as Q.M.S. to date 5/5/18. Auth. A.G.R.M. letter No.9938/18 of 29/5/18. Goo cases admitted 6pm to 6pm – 3 O.R.	nil
"	2/6/18	6pm	Goo cases admitted 6pm to 6pm – 7 Offrs and 26 O.R.	nil
"	3/6/18	6pm	No.S/9793 Pte J. HARTLEY posted to "B" R.N.L.I. for duty and to Join at the Strength of that unit. Received No.1 – 4 NCOS & Men of 65" (R.N.) Division. marched No.1 + 4 NCOS + 9 men. Goo Cases admitted 6pm to 6pm – 32 O.R.	nil
"	4/6/18	6pm	" – 9 O.R.	nil
"	5/6/18	6pm	130 Infants 3 38 Div. J.T.R. over the Y Corps rear centre relief completed 5pm. Field Ambulance moved to HERISSART. Major POWER McR[...] Granted 14 days leave to England. 5pm. Goo cases admitted 6pm to 6pm – 2 O.R.	nil
HERISSART 7.10.C.4.4.	6/6/18	6pm	Received Personal & Confidential Brigade scale	nil
"	7/6/18	6pm	"	nil
"	8/6/18	6pm	"	nil

WAR DIARY / INTELLIGENCE SUMMARY

Army Form C. 2118.

Instructions regarding War Diaries and Intelligence Summaries are contained in F.S. Regs., Part II. and the Staff Manual respectively. Title pages will be prepared in manuscript.

(Erase heading not required.)

Place	Date	Hour	Summary of Events and Information	Remarks and references to Appendices
HERISSART	9/6/18	9pm	2/Lieut. Frank SUMNER, R.D. MORC.SA. and 2/Lieut WHITE. R.L. MORC. USA. and 2/Lieut SISSFSON. W.W. MORC. USA. joined this unit for duty and taken on the Strength from 9/6/18.	
"	10/6/18	6pm	Received Warning Order. 4 mens N.S P.S/325	nil
"	11/6/18	6pm	1 N.R. goes to 14 days leave to England	nil
"	12/6/18	6pm	Received Medical unit order No. S6 and Warning notice N.S N.S/3/s	NLR
"	12/6/18	6pm	Routine Parades	NLR
"	13/6/18	6pm	2/Lt. S/330 & 2/Lt. G.R. SCHOLES. awarded Military Medal with 1 Coy. Ruttis no 681 dt 1/6/18. Received 185 A&Q Brigade Supplementary Instructions	NLR
"	14/6/18	6pm	Routine Parades	NLR
"	15/6/18	6pm	Routine Parades	nil
"	16/6/18	6pm	2/Lieut COSTANZO. MORC. USA reported this unit from DRAKE. B= and to taken on the Strength from 16th inst.	RLLR
"	17/6/18	6pm	Routine Parade	nil
"	18/6/18	6pm	Routine Parade	NLR
"	19/6/18	6pm	Routine Parade	NLR

WAR DIARY

INTELLIGENCE SUMMARY

Army Form C. 2118.

Place	Date	Hour	Summary of Events and Information	Remarks and references to Appendices
HERISSART	20/6/18	6 pm	Received 63rd R.N.D. Medical orders No.s 58 and 59 dated 20/6/18. No S/3044 Sgt CHEETHAM. L.: No S/3053. Sgt THATCHER. J.H. detailed to attend a Gas Course at V Corps Gas school commencing 24th inst.	Nil
"	21/6/18	6 pm	10 Reinforcements received and taken on the strength from 21st No. 63 (RN) Div Inspected the transport & all ranks of 188 Infy Brigade	nil
"	22/6/18	6 pm	G.O.C. 63 (RN) Div inspected the transport & all ranks of 188 Infy Brigade. Major CLARKE M.C. Rams C, 1st/Lieut SISSERSON, and 2nd/Lieut SUMNER with Field Ambulance and on tent subsection left over Charge of the forward Medical post to A.D.S. at MAILLY. MAILLET. and dressing station at BEAUSART. P.r.d.6.6. P.11.6.3.4. from 53rd "70 Amb 17 Div received 63rd R.N.D. medical arrangements No 6. ? 22/6/19.	Nil
ACHEUX P.13.d.4.3	23/6/18	6 pm	Adv Qrs of the Field Amb. moved to ACHEUX and took over the main dressing station from 53rd "70 Amb all ranks in the formand area and at main dressing station completed by 9 A.M. The following personnel then went for temporary duty. Major SCALES McRyan from 150th R.N. F. Amb:- Major ALLISON RANKE Capt CLARKE and 2nd Lieut BROWN. B.S. M.O.R.C and one section of 149 (RN) F Amb. were attached to 3rd Army Rest Camp:- 2 O.R. and Rank No 2 Coy Divisional for temporary duty	Nil

(A7091). Wt. W12859/M1293. 75,000. 1/17. D.D. & L., Ltd. Forms/C.2118-14.

Army Form C. 2118.

WAR DIARY
or
INTELLIGENCE SUMMARY.
(Erase heading not required.)

Place	Date	Hour	Summary of Events and Information	Remarks and references to Appendices
ACHEUX P.13.d.4.3	24/6/18	6pm	Receiving & evacuating sick from the forward area.	A.d.R.
"	25/6/18	6pm	No.S/3450. Cpl. LEWIS.A. - No.S/3392. Pte LEVY.M. No.S/3362 Pte OGDEN.A. No.S/3383. Pte LEA.W.H. posted to 2/1/13=RMLI. and an Church of the Strength of the Unit. Major. POWE R.A.M.C. returned from leave to England. No.S/3371. Cpl MARTIN.J. granted 8 days leave to P+R.I.S. Received 63= R.N.D. warning order No. 90 dated 25/6/18	A.d.R. A.d.R. A.d.R.
"	26/6/18 6pm	27/6/18 6pm	Major SCALES. M.C. R.A.M.C. returned 150 Z.N.M.l. for duty Receiving & evacuating sick from the forward area.	A.d.R.
"	28/6/18	6pm	Lieut COSTANZO. M.O.R.C. U.S.A. reported from Company Aux. with ANSON. Bn.	A.d.R.
"	29/6/18	6pm	Lieut SISSERSON. M.O.R.C. U.S.A. posted to 3 (R.N.) reception Camp "B" for temporary duty.	A.d.R.
"	30/6/18	6pm	Receiving & evacuating sick from the forward area.	A.d.R.

A. R. Hunter
Lieut-Colonel, R.A.M.C.
Commanding (R.N.) Field Ambulance.

CONFIDENTIAL.　　　　　　　　　　　　　　　　　　MEDICAL.

WAR DIARY

of the

148th (Royal Naval) Field Ambulance.

for the period.

1st. July, 1918 to
31st. July, 1918.

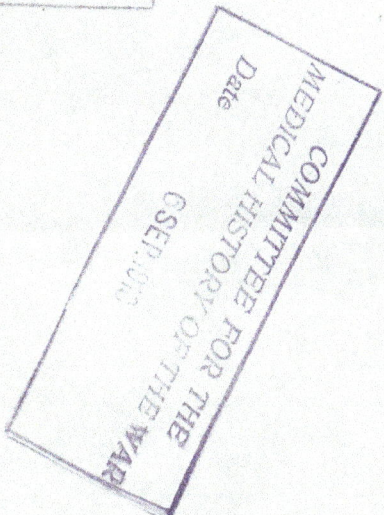

J. Clarke Major, R.A.M.C.,
A/O.C., 148th (R.N.) Field Ambulance.

Army Form C. 2118.

WAR DIARY
or
INTELLIGENCE SUMMARY.
(Erase heading not required.)

Instructions regarding War Diaries and Intelligence Summaries are contained in F. S. Regs., Part II. and the Staff Manual respectively. Title pages will be prepared in manuscript.

Place	Date	Hour	Summary of Events and Information	Remarks and references to Appendices
ACHEUX R.13.d.4.3	1/7/18	6pm	T/211062 Temp S.S.M. CARTER. A.S.C., T/3665 S/Sgt. T. TEAGUE. A.S.C. - T3/023299 S/Sgt BAVERSTOCK. W. joined this unit for duty and are taken on the strength accordingly	R.C.M.
"	2/7/18	6pm	T/141879 S.S.M. GREGGINS. A.S.C. proceeded to Coy Sn Train	R.C.M.
"	3/7/18	6pm	T.S/14109 Sgt COLLINS. C. A.S.C. to No 4 Coy Sn Train. T3/202862 Sgt C.M. WELHAM. to No 1 Coy Sn Train	R.C.M.
"	4/7/18	6pm	Continuing evacuating sick & wounded from the forward area.	R.C.M.
"	5/7/18	6pm	No.S/3979 Pte BLAKELEY. posted to 7th Bn R.M.L.I. and to strike off the strength of this unit from 3/7/18.	R.C.M.
"	6/7/18	6pm	Pte E. COSTANZO. 25. N.O.R.C. granted leave in France for 5 days. No.S/3063 Sgt J.H. THATCHER & S/3784 S/L CHEETHAM. rejoined this unit from 5 Corps Gas School.	R.C.M.
"	7/7/18	6pm	Continuing evacuating wounded from the forward area.	R.C.M.
"	8/7/18	6pm	" "	R.C.M.
"	9/7/18	6pm	No.219735 Pte W. HARTLEY, R.A.M.C. admitted to this unit and is taken on the strength. Revised administrative instructions No 14 d 8/7/18 from today.	R.C.M.

(47929) Wt. W12859/M1393 75,000. 1/17. D.D. & L., Ltd. Forms/C.2118/14.

WAR DIARY
or
INTELLIGENCE SUMMARY.

(Erase heading not required.)

Army Form C. 2118.

Place	Date	Hour	Summary of Events and Information	Remarks and references to Appendices
ACHEUX P13 d.4.B.	10/7/18	6 pm	Collecting & Evacuating Sick & Wounded from the Forward Area	AAR
"	11/7/18	6 pm	"	AAR
"	12/7/18	6 pm	Received Med. Arrangements of 65 Div. A.A. N° 29 Adms N° 8/355. Evacuation will take place by motor B—. 11 KD Wounded	AAR
"	13/7/18	6 pm	Received T.89. Pte Bergam Doctor N° 50. S/3431 Pte J. Hampton. Wounds from the Line, same sent to station on the Shim Rly. One P.O.W. died at A.D.S mainly from shrapnel & shrapnel Gas (British)	AAR
"	14/7/18	6 pm	N° S/3232 Pte J.M. Law. Evacuated to C.C.S (wounded).	AAR
"	15/7/18	6 pm	13 Reinforcements had just joined and taken on the strength	AAR
"	16/7/18	6 pm	A.D.s shelled with modus Gas —	AAR
"	17/7/18	6 pm	Collecting & Evacuating Sick & Wounded in Forward Area —	AAR
"	17/7/18	6 pm	Received Adms Order N° 91.	AAR

Place	Date	Hour	Summary of Events and Information	Remarks and references to Appendices
ACHEUX R.15.d.4.3.	18/7/18	6 pm	Took over duties on the line from R.g. F.A. including a Collecting Post & Car post at Englebelmer.	
"	19/7/18	10 pm	Reinf: 1 S.B., 2 nursing orderlies, Brigade order No. 20 g. received. No. S/30677 Staff S/Sgt C. Brooke & S/3081 Pte W. Bowes granted leave to Paris.	A/DMS.
"	20/7/18	9:30 pm	1 Lieut R.L. WHITE, No 1 RC VS. transferred to C.C.S. (sick). 1 Lieut R.E. COSTANZO. 2. O.R. sent to E. nurses Rest Camp.	A/DMS. A/DMS.
"	21/7/18	6 pm	No 1 RCVS to move Bn HQ for temp. duty.	A/DMS.
"	23/7/18	6 pm	Received returns & order No 52. also hut annex permit No. 5.	A/DMS.
"	25/7/18	9 pm	2 O.R. granted leave to England.	A/DMS.
"	27/7/18	6 pm	Itinerary route No 8. P.A. coming to take over working of formation.	A/DMS. Relief complete 6 pm.

Army Form C. 2118.

WAR DIARY
or
INTELLIGENCE SUMMARY.
(Erase heading not required.)

Instructions regarding War Diaries and Intelligence Summaries are contained in F. S. Regs., Part II. and the Staff Manual respectively. Title pages will be prepared in manuscript.

Place	Date	Hour	Summary of Events and Information	Remarks and references to Appendices
ACHEUX P15d 4·3	25/7/18	6 PM	Advanced party 148 (RN) Field Amb proceed to 63 (RN) Div Rest Station L'MENAGE	Tub
LE MENAGE	26/7/18	6 PM	Took over working of 63 (RN) Div Rest Station at LE MENAGE from the OC 149 (RN) Field Amb. One OR reinforcement joined the unit & taken on the strength	Tub
"	27/7/	6 PM	1st Lieut Sisserson M.O.R.C.; U.S.A. rejoined the unit from Temp Duty at H. 63(RN) Div Rurplion Camp. B. Capt (a/Lieut Colonel) R.T.C. Robertson DSO proceed on 30 days leave of absence to England authority 3rd Army No AC/5-1/890D dated 22/7/18. Capt (a/major) T.W.Clarke M.C. took over command of 148(RN) Field Amb during the absence of Capt (a/Lieut Col) R.T.C. Robertson DSO on leave	Tub
"	28/7/18	6 PM	Received ADMS 63 Div order No 93	Tub
"	29/7/18	6 PM	Took over working of IV Corps Rest Station at Mont RENAULT Fm LENS 11 S·C 15·85 from OC 2/2 WESSEX Field Amb 57th Division	Tub
Mont RENAULT FARM LENS 11 S·C	30/7/18	6 PM	1st Lieut Sisserson M.O.R.C, USA proceed for Temp Duty to 63(RN) Divisional D.A.C. Medical arrangements No 6	Tub

WAR DIARY
or
INTELLIGENCE SUMMARY.

Army Form C. 2118.

Place	Date	Hour	Summary of Events and Information	Remarks and references to Appendices
MONT RENAULT FARM LENS S.C	31/4/19	6 PM	1/Lieut PADDOCK MORC, USA joined this unit & taken on the strength. Wilcocks Major RAMC O/C (R.N.) Field Ambts 148	Sub

148TH (ROYAL NAVAL) FIELD AMBULANCE.

Confidential. Medical.

WAR DIARY
of the
148th (Royal Naval) Field Ambulance
for the period
1st. August, 1918 to 31st. August, 1918.

Lieut.-Col. R.A.M.C.,
Commanding 148th (R.N.) Field Ambulance.

Army Form C. 2118.

WAR DIARY
or
INTELLIGENCE SUMMARY.
(Erase heading not required.)

Instructions regarding War Diaries and Intelligence Summaries are contained in F. S. Regs. Part II. and the Staff Manual respectively. Title pages will be prepared in manuscript.

Place	Date	Hour	Summary of Events and Information	Remarks and references to Appendices
MT RENAULT FARM (Lens H.5°C)	1-8-18	6PM	1st Lieut R.E. COSTANZO (MORC USA) reported this unit from detailed duty with HOOD Battalion received 63 (RN) Div warning order No 94	Nil
"	2-8-18	6PM	Field Amb took over the working of 63 (RN) Div Rest Station at LE MENAGE	Nil
"	3-8-18	6PM	Routine	Nil
"	4-8-18	6PM	No 17844 Acting S/t-major W.A. CLENSHAW RAMC to be temporary S/t-major (warrant officer class I) from 16th March 1918 authority RAMC Records supplementary Corps orders dated 1st June 1918. Received 63 (RN) Div medical unit order No 95 + medical arrangements No 7 Major G.F. ALLISON RAMC reported 149 (RN) Field Amb for duty	Nil
"	5-8-18	6PM	Routine	Nil
"	6-8-18	6PM	Handed over the working of the IV Corps rest station M^d RENAULT FARM to the 2/3 West Riding Field Amb 62 Division. Headquarters of 63 (RN) Div Field Amb moved to 63 (RN) Div Rest Station LE. MENAGE	Nil
LE. MENAGE	7-8-18	6PM	2 O Rs granted 14 days leave to ENGLAND.	Nil
"	8-8-18	6PM	3 O Rs do do	Nil

Army Form C. 2118.

WAR DIARY
or
INTELLIGENCE SUMMARY.

(Erase heading not required.)

Instructions regarding War Diaries and Intelligence Summaries are contained in F. S. Regs., Part II. and the Staff Manual respectively. Title pages will be prepared in manuscript.

Place	Date	Hour	Summary of Events and Information	Remarks and references to Appendices
E MENAGE	9-8-18	6 PM	Field Amb moved to CONTAY U.26.b.2.8 Sheet 57D & joined 188 Inf Brigade Group. 1 St Lieut S.M. MORRIS (MORC USA) taken on the strength of this unit from today's date.	Tub.
CONTAY U.26.b.2.8 Sheet 57 D	10-8-18	6 PM	Received 63 (RN Div) med all arrangements No 8	Tub.
"	11-8-18	6 PM	Routine	Tub.
"	12-8-18	6 PM	Routine	Tub.
"	13-8-18	6 PM	5 ORs granted 14 Days leave to ENGLAND	Tub.
"	14-8-18	6 PM	1 St Lieut MORRIS (MOCC USA) joined this unit from leave in FRANCE	Tub.
"	"	10 PM	Field amb moved with 188 Brigade Group to HÉNU WOOD O.16.d Sheet 57 D	Tub.
HÉNU WOOD O.16.d Sheet 57 D	15-8-18	6 PM	Routine	Tub.
"	16-8-18	6 PM	Routine	Tub.
CITEDELLE DOULLENS	17-8-18	6 PM	Headquarters of F.A. moved to CITEDELLE DOULLENS & General Emanuel Post Station. One section in charge of Major Owen MC remained with 188 Infantry Brigade group.	Tub.

Army Form C. 2118.

WAR DIARY
or
INTELLIGENCE SUMMARY.

(Erase heading not required.)

Instructions regarding War Diaries and Intelligence Summaries are contained in F. S. Regs., Part II. and the Staff Manual respectively. Title pages will be prepared in manuscript.

Place	Date	Hour	Summary of Events and Information	Remarks and references to Appendices
CITADELLE DOULLENS	18-8-18	6 PM	Routine	
"	19-8-18	6 PM	Recd ADMS order No F6/734 dated 19-8-18 HQ of FA rejoined 188 Inf Brigade C24c.3.5 Sh 57D Group at HENU WOOD	
HENU WOOD C24c.3.5	20-8-18	6 PM	5 ORs granted 14 days leave to England. HQs + transport of FA moved to D26c Sh 57D. Advanced Headquarters established with Brigade Group at SOUASTRE. Recd ADMS administration instruction No 23/339 dated 20-8-18 " 63 Div med operation order No 99 dated 20-8-18.	
D26 & Sh.57D	21-8-18	6 PM	Advance HQ of FA moved to ESSARTS. Evacuated Sick & wounded from the forward area. Two ORs of personnel wounded in action.	
"	22-8-18	6 PM	Two other ranks granted leave to England. Recvd ADMS order No 102 dated 22-8-18 Headquarters + transport of FA moved to CITADELLE DOULLENS. 5 ORs of personnel wounded in action. DRS remained with Advanced 5th FA until further orders. FDCD MORRIS MORE USA joined 188 Inf Brigade.	
CITADELLE DOULLENS	23-8-18	6 PM	Prepared to move forward to 10 A.M. Advanced HQ of FA with 188 Inf Brigade moved to ABLAINZEVELLE. Major Town + 1 OR team of personnel wounded in action. Lieut Sassman MORCUSA joined 63 DAC for duty.	
"	24-8-18	6 PM	Advanced HQ of FA moved with 188 Inf Brigade South to G.14.c.9.5.	
"	25-8-18	6 PM	Evacuated Sick + wounded from forward area	
"	26-8-18	6 PM	6 ORs wounded in action + S39151 Pte ASHWORTH.H. of 4th/7A died of wounds at 150th FA Main Dressing Station.	
"	27-8-18	6 PM	S3167 Pte BINGHAM. F. Killed in action + 2 OR personnel wounded. The detachment of FA at LE MENAGE joined HQ at CITADALLE DOULLENS with DRS patients.	

Army Form C. 2118.

WAR DIARY
or
INTELLIGENCE SUMMARY.

(Erase heading not required.)

Place	Date	Hour	Summary of Events and Information	Remarks and references to Appendices
CITADELLE DOULLENS	28-8-18	12 Noon	Lieut Col R.T.C. Roberton DSO returned from leave to England. Advanced H.Q. of F.A. moved with 188 Inf Brigade Group to R3C7.3 Sh51D.	Pub.
"	28-8-18	6pm	Routine:- Major Clarke M.C. arrived at H.Q. Q of F.A. from advanced H.Q. Q of F.A.	R.R.
"	29-8-18	6pm	Major Power M.C. arrived at H.Q. Q of F.A. from advanced H.Q. Q of F.A. and Major Robertson took over charge of Advanced H.Q. F.A. at R3C7.3 Sh51 5YD.	R.R.
"	30-8-18	6pm	Routine:- Evacuating sick from forward area. Received training note from 1SP.	R.R.
"	31-8-18	6pm	Brigade to move. 188 Inf. Brigade at 1 am to BOIRY-ST RICTRUDE and bivetts at S in Station of BOISLEUX-AU-MONT meet Reenft, arriving there at 6 am.	R.R.

....
LIEUT.-COLONEL, R.A.M.C.
COMMANDING 1/1 (R.N.) FIELD AMBULANCE.

148TH
(ROYAL NAVAL)
FIELD AMBULANCE

CONFIDENTIAL.

MEDICAL WAR DIARY

of

148th. (ROYAL NAVAL) FIELD AMBULANCE.

From :-   1st. September 1918.

To :-   30th. September 1918.

[signature]
Lieut. Colonel R.A.M.C.,
Commanding 148th. (R.N.) Field Ambulance.

Army Form C. 2118.

WAR DIARY
or
INTELLIGENCE SUMMARY.
(Erase heading not required.)

Instructions regarding War Diaries and Intelligence Summaries are contained in F. S. Regs., Part II. and the Staff Manual respectively. Title pages will be prepared in manuscript.

Place	Date	Hour	Summary of Events and Information	Remarks and references to Appendices
BOIRY-ST. RICTRUDE thisRef: S.9.C. Sheet 57.B.S.W.	1/9/18	6pm	Fwd Ambulance less attachment working DRS at Citadel Doullens, moved with 188 Infy Brigade from BOIRY-ST. RICTRUDE at 6 pm to FONTAINE-LES-CROISILLES Map Ref. N7-D Sheet 57 B.S.W. arriving at 2 AM. 2/9/18.	R.W.R
CAGNICOURT V.13.C.3.5. Sheet 51.B	2/9/18	6 pm	Fwd Ambulance moved from FONTAINE at 10am with 188 Infy Brigade, VIA CHERISY-HENDECOURT to CAGNICOURT at V.13.C.3.5. arriving 1pm and attached a collecting and car post for 188 Infy Brigade, also established a Relay post at V.20.Central. Casualties were collected and brought to evacuating Amb post at V.13.C.3.5. and evacuated by Cars to A.D.S. at HENDECOURT. 1st Lieut R. PADDOCK, M.O.R.C. US was to to Anson Bn Vii Sing R.K.SHAW (wounded). 5 OR. sent as Reinforcements and taken on the strength of this unit. 8/4/12. Pte W. HALL. 148 ZA mt. wounded.	R.W.R
CAGNICOURT V.13.C.8.4 Sheet 51.B.	3/9/18	6 pm	Nº P.O. 143809 SstMajor G.L. BARFIELD. R.M.L.I. joined the unit as SstMajor and was taken on the strength. Fwd amb. moved from V.13.C.3.5. at 10am with 188 Infy Brigade to a post on the road side at V.15.C.8.4. and remained there receiving Casualties including German wounded	R.W.R

WAR DIARY
or
INTELLIGENCE SUMMARY.

Army Form C. 2118.

Place	Date	Hour	Summary of Events and Information	Remarks and references to Appendices
V.15.C.8.4 Sheet 51B	4/9/18	6pm	Collecting & evacuating wounded of 188 Inf/Brigade to A.D.S. at CASNICOURT.	R.C.R.
"	5/9/18	5pm	Received A.D.M.S. order No. 1 D.S.T. detachment working the M.D.S. at Ataquel DOULLENS. Closed D.R.S. and moved to BEAUMETZ-LES-LOGES. Arriving at midnight.	R.C.R.
"	6/9/18	6pm	Collecting & evacuating casualties from forward area.	R.C.R.
"	7/9/18	6pm	Received A.D.M.S. order No. 106:- The Field Ambulance, less detachment at BEAUMETZ, moved at 2pm to CROISILLES arriving there with 158 Infy Brigade Group at 7pm when Field Amb bivouaced for the night.	R.C.R.
Gov J EN ARTIS	8/9/18	6pm	Detachment of Field Amb. moved from BEAUMETZ-LES-LOGES at 3pm to Gov J EN ARTIS arriving at 4.30pm and Field Amb from CROISILLES arrived by route march at Gov at 9pm when the whole of Field Ambulance was united.	R.C.R.
Gov J EN ARTIS	9/9/18	8am	8 Reinforcements arrived from the Base and are taken on the strength of the Field Amb :- Collecting Sick from Brigade Groups.	R.C.R.

WAR DIARY or INTELLIGENCE SUMMARY

Army Form C. 2118.

Place	Date	Hour	Summary of Events and Information	Remarks and references to Appendices
Gezy.En.ARMS.	10/9/18	6pm	Received from A.D.M.S. Medical arrangements No 11, Collecting Sub Zone Brigade Orders	R.W.R
"	11/9/18	6pm	3. O.R. Granted leave to the United Kingdom	R.W.R
			1 Lieut. PADDOCK U.S.M.O.R.C. is Struck off strength of this Unit and Posted from ANSON Bn. for duty	
			2. Inst. on being Posted to ANSON Bn. for duty	
"	12/9/18	6pm	3 Other Granted leave to England. One OR reinforcement joined the Unit now taken on the Strength from 11/9/18.	R.W.R
"	13/9/18	6pm	2. O.R. Granted leave to England	R.W.R
"	14/9/18	6pm	Routine	R.W.R
"	15/9/18	6pm	Received 188 Inf. Brigade Warning order No. S.C.Q/542 and form S.63 (Bn) Bn order No 107	R.W.R
"	16/9/18	6pm	Received 188 Inf. Brigade order No BM/210 – unit march table attached	R.W.R
BLAIRVILLE X4.a.7.3 Sheet 51C	17/9/18	6pm	Zero Hour moved with R.C.E. Inf. Brigade Group & reached BLAIRVILLE at 2pm and Bivouac for the night	R.W.R

WAR DIARY or INTELLIGENCE SUMMARY

Army Form C. 2118.

Place	Date	Hour	Summary of Events and Information	Remarks and references to Appendices
U.25.a. Sheet 51B	18/9/18	6pm	Field Amb. moved with 188 Infy Brigade Group from BLARGVILLE and arrived at U.25.a Sheet 51B at 6pm and took over Fwd Amb. site that Received 63 RND medical arrangements No 17	NER
U.25.a. Sheet 57B	19/9/18	6am	2 other ranks leave to England	NER
"	"	6pm	Routine	NER
"	20/9/18	6pm	Routine. Lieut R.E. COSTANZO. 15 More poles to XVII Corps for temporary duty	NER
"	21/9/18	6pm	One 4th reinforcement sin Frain taken on the strength	NER
"	22/9/18	6pm	Routine	NER
"	23/9/18	6pm	N2 S/3372. S/Sgt S.F. CHAMBERLAIN, G. awarded a bar to military medal S/3198 L/Cpl C. MAUNDRILL awarded a bar to M.M. S/236.B. Pte STEPHENSON. awarded "M.M." - M/150172. Pte T. ELLWOOD awarded M.M. Auth. 63 (RN) D.R.D. No 4464 of 24/9/18 Lieut C.F. CURTIS, RAMC posted to this unit and taken on the strength and attached to XVII Corps for temporary duty. Received Quartermaster No 108.63 RND	NER
"	24/9/18	6pm	N2 S/3971, Pte H.N. ANDERTON. and N2 S/3937. Pte S. HOLT. and DM2/136228 Sgt C.B. MILLER. A.S.C. Att. Awarded M.M.s. Auth. 14 Corps Letter No A 6/588 dated 1/9/18. Received Tactical arrangements to No 13 (of nineteen)	NER

WAR DIARY
INTELLIGENCE SUMMARY.
(Erase heading not required).

Army Form C. 2118.

Place	Date	Hour	Summary of Events and Information	Remarks and references to Appendices
V.25.A Sheet 57B	25/9/18	6pm	1/Lieut. R.D. SUMNER. I.S.M.O.R.C. posted to Anson Bn for duty and is struck off the strength of this unit.	RWR
			1/Lieut. R.E. COSTANZO M.O.R.C. U.S. evacuated to C.C.S sick and is struck off the strength of this unit.	
			N⁰ S/3438. Pte G. PLATT awarded M.M. Auth 4th Corps Letter N⁰ S8/61A. dd 22/9/18.	
J.4.C. Sheet 57C	26/9/18	6pm	Field Amb moved to J.4.C. LOUVERVAL and formed an Advanced Dressing Station. Major T.W. CLARKE and Juniors moved forward with 188 Infy Brigade.	RWR
J.4.C. Sheet 57C	27/9/18	6pm	Relief Operations Commenced 5=20 A.M. An A.D.S. was established alongside A.D.S of 62 Divisonal at D.15.6.8 Sheet 57c for the free passage of the Devonshire and returned going through this locality. Probably by 62 Divison. Relay post moved to E.14.d.5.4 and Chayfoot established in MOEUVRES at E.14.C.3.4. Advanced Dressing Station moved to E.15.C.55 over canal bank. Casualties through A.D.S to 6pm : 17 Officers and 3 24 other ranks. 2 other Ranks of 146 (RN) + 149 + 7 Amb. wounded	RWR
E.29.a.6.8 Sheet 57C (Sugar factory)	28/9/18	6pm	A.D.S located at Sugar factory at 5am and Relay and Car post established at L.3.a.9.5. Sheet 57 N.E. Casualties passed through A.D.S Officers/ORanks 202.	RWR

Army Form C. 2118.

WAR DIARY
or
INTELLIGENCE SUMMARY.
(Erase heading not required.)

Place	Date	Hour	Summary of Events and Information	Remarks and references to Appendices
ANNEX F2.S.a.3.7 Sheet 51.S.	29/9/16	6pm	Advanced Dressing Station Established at ANNEX, F2.5.a.3.7 Sheet 51.S. Relay post moved to F.18.d.3.7 and car post to L.3. a.9.5. Relay post moved to F29.b.5.5 and car post to F2.S a.5.7 Casualties 6.6 pm. Officer 1, other Ranks 175. Casualty in line personnel 150 (RN) F7.Amb. One O.Rank	MWR
"	30/9/16	6pm	A.D.S. at F25.a.3.7. ANNEX, Car post at F29.b.4.6 Relay post at F.30.a.cent. Section of Regimental Aid Posts. (186 Inf Brigade) 1/8th RMLI. F30 C.1.9. Anson Bn F30.a.9.7 2 Royal Marsh F30.a.5.5 Hawke Bn A.26 C cent. Sheet 51.E. Drake Bn A.25.a.9.7 Sheet 51.Y Bn Hood Bn F.24 C.6.1 51.C (189 Inf Brigade) (190 Inf Brigade) 1 Royal Fusiliers A.26 Cent Sheet 51.C 1/ Robert Rgt to A.26.C.6.6. Sheet 51.E NW. 1 Bedfords A.26 a.1.5 Relay post at F.30.a.cent moved to F.30.a.6.5. and R.A.P of R.Marine Bn moved from F.30.C.1.9 to A.20.C.1.0 (Sheet 51.Y Bn) Total casualties passed through A.D.S 6 to 6pm Officers 8 other Ranks 417. Casualties in Medical personnel : 150 (RN) F.Amb. 3 O.R. Three other Ranks Graves Gave to England.	MWR

A.R.White
Lieut.-Colonel R.A.M.C.
COMMANDING 1/6 (R.N.) FIELD AMBULANCE

Confidential.   Medical.

                                                148TH
                                             (ROYAL NAVAL)
                                            FIELD AMBULANCE.

           W A R   D I A R Y
                of the
       148th (Royal Naval) Field Ambulance.
              for the period
           1st. October, 1918
                   to
                       31st. October, 1918.

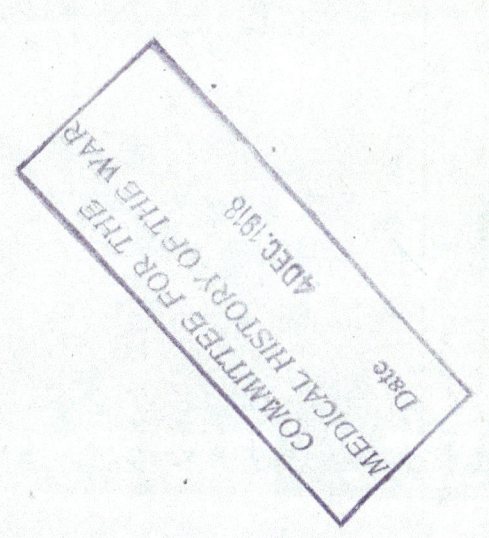

                              M. Clarke Major. R.A.M.C.,
   31st. October, 1918.   A/O.C., 148th (R.N.) Field Ambulance.

WAR DIARY
or
INTELLIGENCE SUMMARY.

Army Form C. 2118.

Place	Date	Hour	Summary of Events and Information	Remarks and references to Appendices
ANNEUX 7.2.S.a.3.6 Sheet 57	1/10/18	6pm	The 1/1 Holland Field Ambulance 52nd Division arrived 1 pm and took over the advanced work and Advanced Dressing Station. Relief completed 6pm. Casualties to completion of relief. Officers 7. and 73 other Ranks	over
"	2/10/18	6pm	Capt. C.K. LISTER. A.A.M.C. joined the Unit and to taken on the strength from 2/10/18.	nil
"	3/10/18	6pm	Routine — Condition of Brigade Sick	nil
"	4/10/18	6pm	Received SS Arty Brigade Running Order No. 231. H.Q. 4/10/18	nil
"	5/10/18	6pm	Major T.W. CLARKE. MC. assumed Command 7th Ambulance during the temporary absence of Lt.Col. R.T.C. ROBERTSON. DSO. Q/ADMS 63rd R.N. Division	nil
"	6/10/18	6PM	3 Other Ranks granted 14 days leave to England	nil
NOYELLES CHATEAU L.II & S.5 Sheet 57C	7/10/18	6PM	Headquarters of F.A. moved to the Chateau NOYELLES L.II & 575'7 and Collechin. Our advanced dressing station. Major M.A. POWER. M.C. R.A.M.C. moved with 188 Inf Brigade to assault position. Heavy shelling of will H.E. & Gas in vicinity during night 7.8% inch. Received 63rd R.N. Med result arrangements (Operations) No /5— No 110	over

Place	Date	Hour	Summary of Events and Information	Remarks and references to Appendices
NOYELLES	8/10/18	6 PM	Heavy shelling of ADS with Gas + HE during night 7+8th. 3 Sunbeam Ambulances + 2 Ford Ambulances damaged by shell fire at the ADS + put out of action. Zero hour was at 04:30 hours. The wounded commenced to arrive at ADS at 06:00 hours. Nine Motor Ambulances arrived at ADS to evacuate cases. First 3 arrived at 06.00 hours & the others in batches of three every half hour. 4 MAC cars were the first motor vehicles to come to an evacuating of ADS then convoying at 10.00 hours. 3 motor ambs from 3/2 local Lance HA & 7 Div started at 13.30 hours for duty. 2 motor ambs from 73 FA 24 Div arrived at 14.00 hours also on loan. ADS morning orders No 111 for relay issued 18.00 hours. Relief of ADS & forward areas by 73 FA 24 Div completed during the night 8 + 9th. Number of casualties passes through ADS up to 19.30 hours was Officers 27 O.Rs 591. P.O.W. O/2 O.R. 71. Total 691. HQs Field Amb returned to ANNEUX F25-a.3.7. ammuny zephyr. Recent 4 Div Train + 23 Med unit reinforcements all taken on Strength Tel from Enemy DCG	

WAR DIARY
or
INTELLIGENCE SUMMARY.

(Erase heading not required.)

Army Form C. 2118.

Place	Date	Hour	Summary of Events and Information	Remarks and references to Appendices
ANNEUX	9/10/18	6 PM	F.A. moved with 188 Inf Bgde Group to MORCHIES I 6 & Shul 57C + billeted under canvas	Inb
MORCHIES I 6 & Shul 57 C	10/10/18	6 PM	Party attached to 17 Corps Main Dressing station reported this date for duty. Party composed of Lieut Curtis & 20 (O.Rs) 188 Inf Bgde order No 234; One (O.R.) Granted 14 days leave to England.	Inb
"	11/10/18	6 PM	F.A. moved with 188 Inf Bgde Group by Rail & Road to 1st Army Area. Personnel by train arriving in billets at SIRACOURT during night 11-12.	Inb
SIRACOURT	12/10/18	6 PM	Capt D.F.A. NEILSON (RAMC) joined for duty from the Reserve & taken on the strength from todays date. Collecting Brigade Transport of Unit arrived at 18.00 hours having come by road.	Inb
"	13/10/18	6 PM	One Other Rank Granted 14 days leave to England. Received 63 (RN) Div Great arrangements No. 16.	Inb
"	14/10/18	6 PM	Routine	Inb

Army Form C. 2118.

WAR DIARY
or
INTELLIGENCE SUMMARY.
(Erase heading not required.)

Instructions regarding War Diaries and Intelligence Summaries are contained in F. S. Regs., Part II. and the Staff Manual respectively. Title pages will be prepared in manuscript.

Place	Date	Hour	Summary of Events and Information	Remarks and references to Appendices
SIRACOURT	15/10/18	6PM	Routine	Nil
"	16/10/18	6PM	Four ORs Granted leave to 1st Army Rest Camp	Nil
"	17/10/18	6PM	Routine	Nil
"	18/10/18	6PM	Routine	Nil
"	19/10/18	6PM	Lieut CURTIS. (RAMC) detailed for temp duty with 1st Artists Rifles & will proceed from 20th inst	Nil
"	20/10/18	6PM	Lieut CURTIS (RAMC) proceeded to 63 (RN) Divisional Engineers & struck off the strength of this unit from the 20th inst.	Nil
"	21/10/18	6PM	Received 188 Inf Brigade order No 236 and SCR/632 also ADMS medical think order No 1113	Nil
GOUY-EN-TERNOIS	22/10/18	6PM	Fired Amb moved with 188 Inf Brigade Group & billeted in GOUY-EN-TERNOIS. Capt NEILSON (RAMC) proceeded to 42' Bde para for temporary duty	Nil
"	23/10/18	6PM	Capt LISTER (AAMC) reported to OC 149(RN) Field Ambulance for temporary duty. Also one large motor ambulance	Nil
"	24/10/18	6PM	One OR detailed for temp duty at Divisional Baths at BERLENCOURT + M2/051842 Serjeant G.F. PONS, ASC MT reported for duty & this unit & taken on the strength from 23rd inst	Nil

(A2094). Wt. W12839/M1293 75,0 o. 1/17. D. B. & L. Ltd. Forms/C2118/14.

Army Form C. 2118.

WAR DIARY
or
INTELLIGENCE SUMMARY.
(Erase heading not required.)

Instructions regarding War Diaries and Intelligence Summaries are contained in F. S. Regs., Part II. and the Staff Manual respectively. Title pages will be prepared in manuscript.

Place	Date	Hour	Summary of Events and Information	Remarks and references to Appendices
GOUY-EN-TERNOIS	24/10/18	6 PM	Capt LISTER (AAMC) rejoined from Temp duty with 149 (RN) Field Amb & to attend daily to 14th Battalion Worcs Gs Regiment for the treatment of Battalion sick & Sanitary Inspection.	JWG
"	25/10/18	6 PM	Renton. Capt LISTER (RAMC) transferred from 1st Bedford Ry Co. & attach for Emp. duty.	JWG
"	26/10/18	6 PM	(Lieut & Q.M.) C L Williams RM granted 14 days leave to England	JWG
"	27/10/18	6 PM	The following ORs of this unit have been awarded the Military Medal No 95192 L/Cpl M. MEADES. S/3545 Pte H BLACK. S/3957 Pte W. WOOD. M2/051069 Pte W.J. DENYER A.S.C. M.T. Authority 17 Corps Letter 25 AG/606 L Col 23-10-18.	JWG
"	28/10/18	6 PM	One OR granted 14 days leave to England	JWG
"	29/10/18	6 PM	Renton	JWG
"	30/10/18	6 PM	Received 63rd Div Medical Unit Warning order No 1114 & 188 Inf Brigade Warning order No 237.	JWG
"	31/10/18	6 PM	Capt LISTER (AAMC) posted to 14th Worcs Gs Battalion for Emp duty.	JWG

Army Form C. 2118.

WAR DIARY
or
INTELLIGENCE SUMMARY.

(Erase heading not required.)

Place	Date	Hour	Summary of Events and Information	Remarks and references to Appendices
GOUY-EN-TERNOIS	31/10/18	6PM	Received 188 Inf Brigade movement order No 239	Ind.

Webb-Johnson Major RAMC
a/OC 148 (RN) Field Ambulance

[Stamp: 148TH (ROYAL NAVAL) FIELD AMBULANCE. 31/10/18]

Confidential   Medical

War Diary
of the
148th (R.N.) Field Ambulance
for the period

1st November 1918
to
30th November 1918

[Stamp: 148TH (ROYAL NAVAL) FIELD AMBULANCE. No. ___ Date 30/11/18]

[Signature]
Lieut. Col. Raine
O.C. 148 (R.N.) Field Ambulance

Army Form C. 2118.

WAR DIARY
or
INTELLIGENCE SUMMARY.
(Erase leading not required.)

Instructions regarding War Diaries and Intelligence Summaries are contained in F. S. Regs., Part II. and the Staff Manual respectively. Title pages will be prepared in manuscript.

Place	Date	Hour	Summary of Events and Information	Remarks and references to Appendices
EVIN MALMAISON	1/11/18	6PM	Field Ambulance moved by Bus with 188 Inf Brigade. Group & Hieted at EVIN MALMAISON. Transport of Field amb moved by stages by Road.	Feb
"	2/11/18	6PM	Transport Section of Field Amb arrived in Billets at EVIN MALMAISON	Feb
"	3/11/18	6PM	Received 188 Inf Brigade marching orders no 241. One O R proceeded 14 days leave to England.	Feb
"	4/11/18	6PM	First line transport of Field amb moved with 188 Inf Brigade. Capt C.R. LISTER. A.M.C. proceeded to 6 England for duty & to struck off the strength of this unit. Temp Surgeon G.F.B. GILNESTY. R.N. joined & is taken on the strength of this Field Amb from the 3rd inst.	Feb
HAULCHIN	5/11/18	6PM	Field amb moved by Bus with 188 Inf Brigade & Billeted at HAULCHIN. 1st Line Transport of Field amb arrived with personnel.	Feb
AULNOY	6/11/18	6PM	Field Amb moved by Road with 188 Inf Brigade. Group to AULNOY & 1st Line Transport of Field amb. Group & Billeted in rest with rft. with marching orders no 116 & Operation order no D. Q. 27. Received 63 (RN) Div. no D. R. 27. Also 188 Inf Brigade Supplementary report no 5. Supplement no 5.	Feb

Army Form C. 2118.

WAR DIARY
or
INTELLIGENCE SUMMARY.
(Erase heading not required.)

Place	Date	Hour	Summary of Events and Information	Remarks and references to Appendices
SAULTAIN	7/11/18	6 PM	Football and round by Road with 188 Inf Bgde. Band + assisted at SAULTAIN. Kindred Transport accompanied the unit. On OR from Col 14 days special leave to England. Lieut Col R T C ROBERTSON DSO came rejoined the unit and from sicklist duty as acting RAMS and resumed command of this unit from today's date.	Sub.
			Field Ambulance moved from SAULTAIN to SEBOURQUIAUX with 188 Inf Bgde and the Bde Group.	AWR
			On the Route Granted Leave to England	
ANGRE	8/11/18	6pm	Moved with 88 Inf Bgde Group from to ANGRE and established 6 MDSs for the 63rd Division with Convent Main Power W.C. with Bearer division moved forward with 188 Inf Bgde Group.	AWR
			On the Route Granted Leave to England.	
AUDREGNIES	9/11/18	6pm	M.D.S. closed down at ANGRE at 12 noon and opened at the Convent AUDREGNIES.	AWR
			On the Route Granted Leave to England.	

Army Form C. 2118.

WAR DIARY
or
INTELLIGENCE SUMMARY.
(Erase heading not required.)

Place	Date	Hour	Summary of Events and Information	Remarks and references to Appendices
ADDRIGNES	10/11/18	9.0 p.m	Capt Porter. M.O.R.C.U.S. attached to this unit for temporary duty from 149. F.A.	AWR
"	11/11/18	10.0 p.m	Hostilities ceased at 1100 hours today	AWR
"	12/11/18	8 p.m	On the March towards area in England.	
NOUVELLES	13/11/18	6 p.m	Recce Offr of this unit moved to NOUVELLES to open HQ. Inter Personnel moved. Zone requirements - Issued. The unit is en-route on the Stein Pk from 11/11/18 - Major T.W. CLARKE M.C. granted 30 days Special leave to England. Auth Adm S 63 Div. No 25/349. Capt NEILSON. Relinquishes unit from temporary duty with 150 F.A.	AWR

WAR DIARY
or
INTELLIGENCE SUMMARY.

(Erase heading not required.)

Army Form C. 2118.

Instructions regarding War Diaries and Intelligence Summaries are contained in F. S. Regs., Part II. and the Staff Manual respectively. Title pages will be prepared in manuscript.

Place	Date	Hour	Summary of Events and Information	Remarks and references to Appendices
NOUVELLES	14/11/18	6pm	Capt. C.L. WILLIAMS rejoined from leave to England.	nil
"	15/11/18	6pm	Capt. BROWN No R.C.V.S. rejoined 74977 from Turfong. Act. Lo.cl M.S. rank 746 T.A.	nil
"	16/11/18	8pm	A.D.V.S. 63 Div. inspected the Unit in France and delivered an address prior to taking his departure from this Div. as A.D.V.S.	nil
"	17/11/18	6pm	Received 63rd Div Hd Qrs Unit Order No 17	nil
VALENCIENNES	18/11/18	8pm	The Unit this Morning on tent Sub-division moved to Valenciennes and Established a hospital at the LYCEE for the reception of sick & wounded P.O.W.	nil
"	19/11/18	6pm	Routine	nil
"	20/11/18	6pm	Routine	nil
"	21/11/18	8pm	Lieut. GILKES Py. (RN) granted 14 days special leave to England	nil

WAR DIARY
or
INTELLIGENCE SUMMARY.

Army Form C. 2118.

Place	Date	Hour	Summary of Events and Information	Remarks and references to Appendices
MEMBRIES	21/11/16	6.30pm	An Officer & 149 F.A. detailed to H.Q Adm.S. for temporary duty with 146 F.A. detached vice Sergt Gilkes P.V.	nil
"	22/11/16	8pm	General H.S. Horne G.O.C. 1st Army visited the troops	nil
"	23/11/16	6pm	Routine	nil
"	24/11/16	5.30pm	Capt T.O. Clarke MC reported for temporary duty from 149 F.A.	nil
"	"	"	One ot Reinforcement joined the unit and is taken on the Strength	nil
"	25/11/16	5.30pm	R.E. Costanzo Corpl. 15 and 1 Hurst Pte Seamus Sanit Tho unit are taken on the Strength	nil
"	26/11/16	5.30pm	Routine	nil
"	27/11/16	6pm	Routine	nil
"	28/11/16	6pm	Routine	nil
"	29/11/16	5.30pm	Routine	nil
"	30/11/16	5.30pm	Routine	nil

W.A.M.Intosh Lt Col.

LIEUT.-COLONEL, R.A.M.C.
COMMANDING (R.N.) FIELD AMBULANCE.

CONFIDENTIAL.

"AD DIMPY".

MEDICAL.

148th (P.N.) FIELD AMBULANCE.

FROM.................. 1st DECEMBER 1918.

TO.................... 31st DECEMBER 1918.

COMMITTEE FOR THE
MEDICAL HISTORY OF THE WAR
Date 6 MAR 1919

In the field.   Lieut-Col. R.A.M.C.
31.12.18.   Commanding 148th (P.N.) Field Ambulance.

WAR DIARY or INTELLIGENCE SUMMARY

Army Form C. 2118.

Instructions regarding War Diaries and Intelligence Summaries are contained in F. S. Regs., Part II. and the Staff Manual respectively. Title pages will be prepared in manuscript.

(Erase heading not required.)

Place	Date	Hour	Summary of Events and Information	Remarks and references to Appendices
VALENCIENNES	1/1/19	6pm	Major T.A.A. Power M.C. awarded a second bar to Military Cross. Auth: G.3 ORO 4552.	Recd.
"	2/1/19	6pm	Hon. Lieut & Qm. C.L. WILLIAMS R.M. promoted temporary Captain a/ 1/18/18 Auth post'd Orders No. 47.	Recd
"	3/1/19	8pm	Routine with Returned Prisoners of War Con. Camp.	Recd
"	4/1/19	8pm	" " "	Sent
"	5/1/19	7pm	" " "	Recd
"	6/1/19	8pm	Surg. Lieut. H.O. RYDER (RN) joined his unit and is taken on the strength.	Recd
"	7/1/19	6pm	Routine	Recd
"	8/1/19	8pm	QMS B.J.C. KERR appointed a/ssp Major from No.6 Auth No.5/3157. Aq RM Letter No.RM/16787/5- a/11/1/19 and Lee taken on the strength	Recd
"	9/1/19	8pm	1st O.R. joined this unit and is taken on the strength	Recd
"	10/1/19	6pm	Routine	Recd
"	11/1/19	8pm	Pte WHEELER J.H. A.S.C. joined this unit from 65 Div MT Coy. and is taken on the strength. M.T/O/33/5/8	Recd

WAR DIARY
INTELLIGENCE SUMMARY
Army Form C. 2118.

Place	Date	Hour	Summary of Events and Information	Remarks and references to Appendices
VALENCIENNES	11/4/19		The following Honors awarded M-M.M. No S/3052 Sgt A. COVELL No S/393'S Pte A. STOTT. — No S/3950 Pte J. DOWNIE No S/3838 Pte C. EASTWOOD. No 337754 Pte S. ORD. Auth 63rd D.R.O. No 457. 10 OR Coal Miners dispatched to VIII Corps Coal Camp for Demobilization.	AcK
"	13/14 9pm		Coal Miners dispatched to VIII Corps Coal Camp for Demobilization.	AcK
"	14/4 8pm		Reamg. To 3 Div. Movement order No. 119. dated 13/4/18 Pt Kent Ostanzo 6/3rd Brigade R.F.A. for being Struck P.O.W. at 9 am Returning Returned P.O.W. at 9 am	AcK
PATURAGES	14/4/19 10am		Commenced 9 July with 1st Army Brigade and Lalled all Stations in area allotted. 156 Inf Brigade now forms a Hd of Set? Round Front 155 Inf Brigade S.R.	AcK
"	15/4/19 8pm		Lieut Kent had been tried to Hosp B-n and is struck off the Strength of this Unit S.O.B 1st Div AcmtA. 9 am	AcK

WAR DIARY / INTELLIGENCE SUMMARY

Army Form C. 2118.

Place	Date	Hour	Summary of Events and Information	Remarks and references to Appendices
PADRAGES	16/1/18	1/30pm	Fresh orders received from A.D.M.S. XIII Div. One S/F OR established as corps Rest Station at Palmichenne for Convalescents	and
"	17/1/18	3pm	2 O.R. posted to 149 FA. & one car struck off the strength	
"	"	"	2 I.R. & S.C. Servia Rhia unit and entrained on the strength	aerk
"	"	3.30pm	5 O.R. Coal Carriers dispatched to VIII Corps Coal Camp for Demobilisation	
"	"	"	Lieut. Gillespy proceeded to 3rd Brigade for Temp duty.	
"	"	"	Their costanys W.R.C. &c A. proceeded to 25 Eal troops Ann.	
"	"	"	10 Slough off the strength of the Unit	
"	"	"	Lieut Gunner proceeded to 1st Light Rly Workshops, BARUN on 7b struck off the strength of the unit	
"	"	"	5 OR Francis Hann to Enfluency	
"	19/1/18	10am	Mjr. T.W. CLARKE M.C returns from leave rom then to Ek. Rental	RSJR REtR
"	20/1/18	10.30am	Capt NEILSON, Lieut proceeded to 3rd Brigade Rgt. for duty. Lieut GILLESPY (AN) proceeded to No 2 CCS from 3rd Brigade Rgt. for temp duty. - 2 NCOs and 38. OR attached from 32 CCS for temporary duty	REtR REtR RetR

(A7092). Wt. W12839/M203. 75 9.0. 1/17. D. D. & L., Ltd. Forms/C.2118/14.

WAR DIARY or INTELLIGENCE SUMMARY

Army Form C. 2118.

Place	Date	Hour	Summary of Events and Information	Remarks and references to Appendices
PATRAGES	21/9/18	6pm	Routine	AWR
"	22/9/18	6pm	Major Power M.C. granted 14 days leave to UKingdom. O.R. cove numerous dispatches to VIII Corps remount Centre	AWR
"	23/9/18	6pm	Routine	AWR
"	24/9/18	6pm	Capt. NEILSON R.A.M.C. reports the under form being duly with 31 Bon park R.F.A. The following Substantive ranks are authorised by A armies 63 Div S/13064 P/Sjt A. COVELL M.M. to Sjt S/13194 Cpl. C. MAYNDRILL M.M. M.M. to Cple. S/1333 v5 L/Cpl. E.A. GRIEVES - to Cpl.	AWR
"	25/9/18	6pm	O.R. dispatches for VIII Corps remount Centre	AWR
"	26/9/18	6pm	2 O.R. granted leave to England O.R. cove numerous dispatches to VIII Corps Remount Centre	AWR
"	27/9/18	6pm	Routine	AWR
"	28/9/18	6pm	2/SM Turner B.J. CARR and 24 O.R. despatched to Reeny G. Cinc. 2/R VIII Corps.	AWR

Army Form C. 2118.

WAR DIARY
or
INTELLIGENCE SUMMARY.

(Erase heading not required.)

Instructions regarding War Diaries and Intelligence Summaries are contained in F. S. Regs, Part II. and the Staff Manual respectively. Title pages will be prepared in manuscript.

Place	Date	Hour	Summary of Events and Information	Remarks and references to Appendices
PATURAGES	29/4/18	6pm	5th R Coal Miners deputation to VIII Corps Demo & Centre	att.
	30/4/18	10am	G.O.R. 9/13 Bn R.W.F. reports for temp duty with the thanougal	att.
			Return	
	31/4/18	10.30am	Return	att.

A.W.R. Curtis ? Lt. Col.

CONFIDENTIAL. 63rd DIV MEDICAL.

WAR DIARY. Box 2985

148th (Royal Naval) Field Ambulance.

From   1st January 1919.

To   31st January 1919.

@@@@@@@@@@@@@@@@@@

31.1.19.
Lieut-Colonel. R.A.M.C.
Commanding 148th (R.N.) Field Ambulance.

Army Form C. 2118.

WAR DIARY
or
INTELLIGENCE SUMMARY.
(Erase heading not required.)

Instructions regarding War Diaries and Intelligence Summaries are contained in F. S. Regs., Part II. and the Staff Manual respectively. Title pages will be prepared in manuscript.

Place	Date	Hour	Summary of Events and Information	Remarks and references to Appendices
PATURAGES	1/1/19	9.0 am	Recognised Holiday	AWR
"	2/1/19	6 pm	H. OR found as reinforcements and taken on the strength.	AWR
"	3/1/19	6 pm	Routine.	AWR
"	4/1/19	6 pm	H. Hanks proceeded to VIII Corps Con Camp for demobilisation	AWR
"	5/1/19	6 pm	Routine	AWR
"	6/1/19	6 pm	Routine	AWR
"	7/1/19	6 pm	1 O.R. proceeded to VIII C Camp for demobilisation	AWR
"	8/1/19	6 pm	Routine	AWR
"	9/1/19	6 pm	2/Lt Grantis 14 days leave to UK	AWR
"	10/1/19	6 pm	Routine	AWR
"	11/1/19	6 pm	Major Poer M.C. returned from leave to UK	AWR
"	12/1/19	6 pm	2 O.R. to CC for demob.	AWR
"	13/1/19	6 pm	1 O.R. 1 S.C.M.T. Some Dn. inoch ?? taken on the strength	AWR

WAR DIARY
or
INTELLIGENCE SUMMARY.

(Erase heading not required.)

Army Form C. 2118.

Place	Date	Hour	Summary of Events and Information	Remarks and references to Appendices
PATRASES	14/1/19	6pm	1st A.S.C. Camps for Demob.	R.W.R
"	15/1/19	6pm	Routine	R.W.R
"	16/1/19	6pm	Routine	R.W.R
"	17/1/19	6pm	Routine	R.W.R
"	18/1/19	6pm	The following Medals awarded:- M.M.! No S/3054 Sgt COVELL.A M.M. bar to M.M.: No S/3659. Pte PROUD A.T. No S/3357 Pte LORD A. No S/3353 Pte J.CROOK. No S/3625. Pte R. LEE. No M/53466.Pte J.P. WILLIAMS A.S.C. attached. Authority G.S. Div. Routine order dated 15/1/19.	M.M.R
"	19/1/19	6pm	2nd O.R. to VIII Corps C.C. for Demob. - 3rd Grade 74 days leave U.K.	R.W.R
"	20/1/19	6pm	Major M.F. Power M.C. proceeded to VIII Corps Schnechon Centre	R.W.R
"	21/1/19	6pm	No S/3544 Staff Sgt H. Proctor granted Q.M.S+W.O(I) 14/4/16 A.C.I.	R.W.R
"	22/1/19	6pm	2nd O.R. proceeded to VII Corps C.C. for demob. Lieut R.D. Summers Joins this Unit from 1.R.W (Berlin) Returns on strength. 1st A.S.C. M.T. Games this unit & taken on the strength	R.W.R

WAR DIARY
or
INTELLIGENCE SUMMARY.
(Erase heading not required.)

Army Form C. 2118.

Place	Date	Hour	Summary of Events and Information	Remarks and references to Appendices
PATRAGES	23/1/19	6pm	Major M A Power MC returning from Clerk ED Centre - Lieut R D Sumner to RMLI for Dirty	NIL
"	24/1/19	6pm	Routine	NIL
"	25/1/19	6pm	Routine	NIL
"	26/1/19	6pm	V.M. Sanders transf to V.R. J Col RTC Returns agenda A/ADMS 63200 from 27/1/19 to 26/2/19.	NIL
"	27/1/19	6pm	Routine	NIL
"	28/1/19	6pm	Routine	NIL
"	29/1/19	6pm	Routine	NIL
"	30/1/19	6pm	Routine	NIL
"	31/1/19	6pm	Routine	NIL

LIEUT.-COLONEL, R.A.M.C.
COMMANDING (R.N.) FIELD AMBULANCE.

— MEDICAL —

— CONFIDENTIAL —

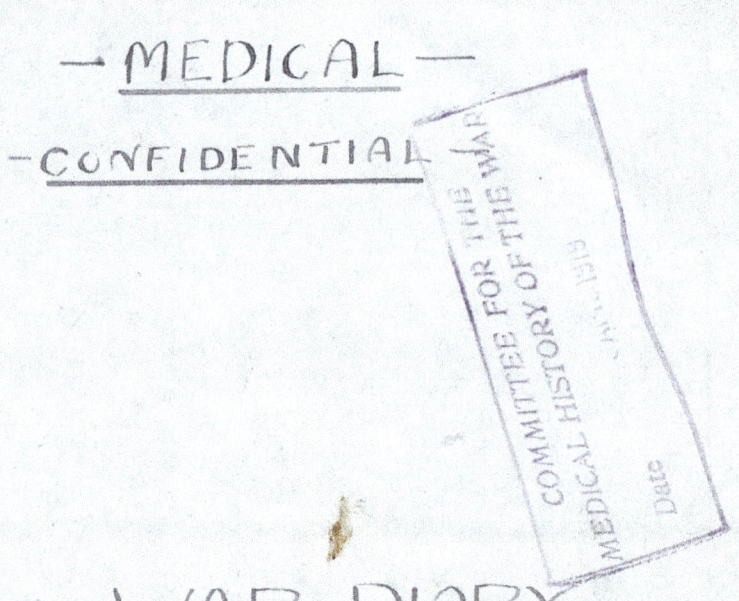

WAR DIARY.

OF

148 (RN) FIELD AMBULANCE

From: 1st February 1919

To: 28th February 1919

—— " ——

28th February 1919.

[signature] Wclarke
MAJOR RAMC.
A/O.C. 148 (RN) FIELD AMBULANCE

Army Form C. 2118.

WAR DIARY
or
INTELLIGENCE SUMMARY.
(Erase heading not required.)

Instructions regarding War Diaries and Intelligence Summaries are contained in F. S. Regs., Part II. and the Staff Manual respectively. Title pages will be prepared in manuscript.

Place	Date	Hour	Summary of Events and Information	Remarks and references to Appendices
PATURAGES	1/1/19	6 pm	3 O. Ranks proceeded to Concent. Camp for demobilization	WAR
"	2/1/19	6 pm	Routine	WAR
"	3/1/19	6 pm	Capt NEILSON. R.A.M.C. granted 14 days leave to U.K. also 5 O Ranks.	WAR
"	4/1/19	6 pm	Routine	WAR
"	5/1/19	6 pm	3 O.R. taken on in strength as reinforcements from base.	WAR
"	6/1/19	6 pm	1 Other granted 14 days leave to U.K. – 5 proceed to Concent. Camp for demobilization.	WAR
			Major F. W. CLARKE. M.C. R.A.M.C. awarded a bar to the M.C. authority D.R.O. 4807. d/4/1/19.	
"	7/1/19	6 pm	Routine	WAR
"	8/1/19	6 pm	Routine	WAR
"	9/1/19	6 pm	3 O.R. proceed to Concentration Camp for demob.	WAR
"	10/1/19	6 pm	The following appointments have been approved S/3432. Pte N. W. HOMER. to a/Sgt Clerk 2/1/19. = S/3194. L/Cpl C. MAUNDRILL h.h. to a/Sgt. G.D. d/1/1/19. S/3539. Pte A. TITLEY to a/Cpl G.D. a/9/12/18. S/4000 Pte J. J. WILMAN. to a/Cpl G.D. a/11/1/19. S/3257. Pte A. LORD. M.M. to a/Sgt G.D. d/1/1/19 auth. ADM S. 58/100. d/31/2/19. Lieut SUMNER M.O.R.C. is returning from duties in duty rank, 2 Br.R.H.L.	WAR

(A7092) Wt W12830/M1293 75,000. 1/17. D. D. & L., Ltd. Forms/C.2118/14.

Army Form C. 2118.

WAR DIARY
or
INTELLIGENCE SUMMARY.
(Erase heading not required.)

Instructions regarding War Diaries and Intelligence Summaries are contained in F. S. Regs., Part II. and the Staff Manual respectively. Title pages will be prepared in manuscript.

Place	Date	Hour	Summary of Events and Information	Remarks and references to Appendices
PATRAGES	11/7/19	6 pm	3 O.R. granted 14 days leave to U.K.	recd
"	12/7/19	6 pm	Routine	recd
"	13/7/19	6 pm	6 O.R. to Concent Camp for Demob	recd
"	14/7/19	6 pm	Routine	recd
"	15/7/19	6 pm	Routine	recd
"	16/7/19	6 pm	Routine	recd
"	17/7/19	6 pm	3 O.R. to Concent Camp for Demob	recd
"	18/7/19	6 pm	Routine	recd
"	19/7/19	6 pm	Other Ranks Concent. with O.C. I.S. proceeded to I.S. of R.N.T.S. for Auscultation	recd
"	20/7/19	6 pm	Routine	recd
"	21/7/19	6 pm	Routine	recd
"	22/7/19	6 pm	Routine: Surg Lieut F.B. Etheridge (R.N.) proceeded to England on report to Admiralty, auth: Shuta C/99 7th Through this Unit. Authority D.Q.M.S. N.Q. 101/14 d/15/7/19. Capt O.? Evans R.A.M.C to Vizces from 63 Brit Receipt Camp	recd Recd

Army Form C.2118.

WAR DIARY
or
INTELLIGENCE SUMMARY.
(Erase heading not required.)

Instructions regarding War Diaries and Intelligence Summaries are contained in F. S. Regs., Part II. and the Staff Manual respectively. Title pages will be prepared in manuscript.

Place	Date	Hour	Summary of Events and Information	Remarks and references to Appendices
PATRAGES	23/2/19	6pm	Routine	nil
"	24/2/19	6pm	3 OR to Convalescent Camp for Observation & Investigation. 2 ORs granted 14 days leave to U.K.	nil
"	25/2/19	6pm	Routine	nil
"	26/2/19	6 PM	Lieut Col R.T.C. Robertson D.S.O. R.A.M.C. granted 14 days leave to U.K. Capt & Major T.W. Clarke M.C. R.A.M.C. takes over command of the Unit during his absence	Inb.
"	27/2/19	6 P.M.	Routine.	Inb.
"	28/2/19	6 P.M.	Routine	Inb.

Tubbarka Major R.A.M.C.
O/C. 146 (P.K.) Field Ambulance

MEDICAL

CONFIDENTIAL

WAR DIARY

OF

148 (RN) FIELD AMBULANCE.

From 1st March 1919.
To. 31st March 1919.

_____ Lt. Col. RAMC.
O.C. 148 (RN) FIELD AMBULANCE

Army Form C. 2118.

WAR DIARY
or
INTELLIGENCE SUMMARY.
(Erase heading not required.)

Instructions regarding War Diaries and Intelligence Summaries are contained in F. S. Regs., Part II. and the Staff Manual respectively. Title pages will be prepared in manuscript.

Place	Date	Hour	Summary of Events and Information	Remarks and references to Appendices
PATURAGES	1-3-19	6PM	Capt. a/major M.A TOWER M.C. posted to 149 F.A. + taken off the strength of the unit from todays date. Capt. G.O.F. ALLEY M.C. taken on the strength from the 2nd Royal Irish Regiments. Lieut. R.D. SUMNER M.C., U.S.A. returned from Allied duty with the 150 F.A. S/3373 S/S STF L/S. TAMBERLIN appointed a/Sergt. major W.O.I. from 27-12-18. Auth. Part II order 212.19. Three other ranks to concentration camp for demobilization.	Enc.
"	2-3-19	6PM	One other rank to concentration camp for demobilization.	Enc.
"	3-3-19	6PM	Routine.	Enc.
"	4-3-19	6PM	Routine.	Enc.
"	5-3-19	6PM	One O.R. granted 14 days special leave to the U.K.	Enc.

Army Form C. 2118.

WAR DIARY
or
INTELLIGENCE SUMMARY.
(Erase heading not required.)

Instructions regarding War Diaries and Intelligence Summaries are contained in F. S. Regs., Part II. and the Staff Manual respectively. Title pages will be prepared in manuscript.

Place	Date	Hour	Summary of Events and Information	Remarks and references to Appendices
PATURAGES	6-3-19	6 PM	Two O.Rs. proceeded to Army of Occupation	Nil
"	7-3-19	"	One O.R. proceeded to Concentration Camp for demobilization	Nil
"	8-3-19	"	Two O.Rs. "	Nil
"	9-3-19	"	Routine	Nil
"	10-3-19	"	S/3040 Serjeant J. HIBBERT appointed acting staff Serjeant from 9-2-19 authority ADMS 58/108 dated 8-3-19	Nil
"	11-3-19	"	Three O.Rs. to Concentration Camp for demobilization	Nil
"	12-3-19	"	Routine	Nil
"	13-3-19	"	One O.R. granted special leave to U.K.	Nil
"	14-3-19	"	Routine	Nil
"	15-3-19	"	Nine O.Rs. proceeded to Con. Camp for Demob.	Nil

WAR DIARY
or
INTELLIGENCE SUMMARY.
(Erase heading not required.)

Army Form C. 2118.

Place	Date	Hour	Summary of Events and Information	Remarks and references to Appendices
PATURAGES	16-3-19	6 PM	Routine	Intd
"	17-3-19	6 PM	S/3221 Pte E STANSFIELD placed in 44 rate of Corps pay as Cook from 25-2-19 authority Part II orders 10-3-19	Intd
"	18/19	6 PM	11097 Pte A.R. Rhuutosh returned from leave to England.	RRR
"	19-3-19	6 PM	3 O.R. taken on Strength as reinforcements from Div Train	RRR
"	20-3-19	6 PM	2 O.R. to Con Camp for demob — S/4258 Pte Hargreaves W.J. & S/... Pte Clinton on 5 Rate of Corps pay as Clerks from 21-2-19. Auth Park 2 orders 17-3-19	RRR
"	21-3-19	6 PM	1 O.R. taken on Strength from Div Train Capt D.J.A Nelson RAMC admitted to No 5 whilst on leave taken off Strength of unit from 15-2-19	RRR
"	22-3-19	6 PM	R.T.O. R.D. Summers Lt.A.M.C. appointed Capt from 13-2-19 with Army Officers War ratio 12-3-19. 1 O.R. taken on Strength from Div Train	RRR
"	23-3-19	6 PM	6 O.R. Posted to 4 + C.C.S for detached duty S/39778 Lt. Col. Dixon. J. taken off Strength as from 3-1-19. Arrival whilst on leave	RRR

Army Form C.2118/14.

WAR DIARY
or
INTELLIGENCE SUMMARY.

(Erase heading not required.)

Army Form C. 2118.

Instructions regarding War Diaries and Intelligence Summaries are contained in F.S. Regs., Part II. and the Staff Manual respectively. Title pages will be prepared in manuscript.

Place	Date	Hour	Summary of Events and Information	Remarks and references to Appendices
DATURHEES	24/3/19	6pm	Routine	NIL
"	25/3/19	6.00am	Routine	NIL
"	26/3/19	9pm	15 O.R. to Con. Camp for Durban. 1 O.R. taken on Strength as Reinforcement from Durban. 1 O.R. proceeded to No.1 Base M.T. Depot for duty	NIL
"	27/3/19	6pm	Surg. Lieut. J.R. Bawdi-Clough (R.N) taken on Strength. Burnt from R.M.L.I. 27-3-19.	NIL
"	28/3/19	6pm	Capt. I. Summer & S.M.C. to England & taken off Strength 28-3-19. Auxt. Adm S. 109/42 21-26-3-19. Capt. G.O.? Alley M.C. R.M.C. proceeded to Adm S. Barcosine for duty and taken off Strength Adm S-109/42	NIL
"	29-3-19	6pm	Routine	NIL
"	30-3-19	6pm	1 O.R. taken on Strength as reinforcement from Durban 15/32 S? Sgt W.G. Bland appointed Armament Officer Class I from 9-2-19 Auxt D.R.O 4989. 28/3/19	NIL

Army Form C. 2118.

WAR DIARY
or
INTELLIGENCE SUMMARY.
(Erase heading not required.)

Place	Date	Hour	Summary of Events and Information	Remarks and references to Appendices
PANTAGES	31/3/19	6pm	3. OR to Con Camps for demob — 1 OR to No 2 C.C.S for duty — 2 OR taken on strength as reinforcements from Div Train. 5 OR returned from detached duty at Valenciennes	

A.R. Anstall ? Col.
LIEUT.-COLONEL R.A.M.C.
COMMANDING 148 C.M.Y CORPS

MEDICAL.
Confidential

140/3550

WAR DIARY

of

148 (Royal Naval) Field Ambulance.

From 1st April 1919
To 30th April 1919.

JMcCarty Capt. RAMC
O/C 148(RN) Field Ambulance.

30/4/19.

WAR DIARY
or
INTELLIGENCE SUMMARY

Army Form C. 2118.

Place	Date	Hour	Summary of Events and Information	Remarks and references to Appendices
PATRAS	1/4/19	6pm	Major T W Clarke OBE Rank proceeds to UK on 5 Staples for duty auth AFW5 10.9/496.d. 31-3-19. 7 OR taken on Strength	MR
"	2/4/19	6pm	Routine	MR
"	3/4/19	6pm	Routine	MR
"	4/4/19	6pm	S/40 31 Pte Brinkman E placed on S Rate of Corps pay from 21-2-19 auth part 2 order 31-3-19. 2 OR to Con Camps for Convalescence	MR
"	6/4/19	6pm	2 OR granted leave to UK from 6/4/19. 10 OR transferred to A.M.T Coy; 7 OR to Con Camps for Convalescence	MR
"	7/4/19	6pm	S. OR to Con Camp for Convalescence = 10 OR transferred to 6th D.M.T Coy	MR
"	8/4/19	6pm	2 OR granted leave to UK from 8/4/19 - Routine	MR
"	9/4/19	6pm	Lt Col A C Rotholz OSO proceeds to UK on Special duty, Major J Lynch takes over Command temporarily and Surg. D.L. Bessemer Clark takes over Command temporarily	MR

WAR DIARY
or
INTELLIGENCE SUMMARY.
(Erase heading not required.)

Army Form C. 2118.

Place	Date	Hour	Summary of Events and Information	Remarks and references to Appendices
Petrograd	10.4.19	6 PM	Capt I.M. McCulfe reported for Duty from the 37th Divn on other rank to 63rd BMD Corps By for Almost	7 h.m.
"	11.4.19	6 PM	Routine	7 h.m.
"	12.4.19	6 PM	Routine	7 h.m.
"	13.4.19 6 PM		Routine. 3 other ranks granted leave to the United Kingdom 3	7 h.m.
"	14.4.19	6 PM	From other rank to 16.3 "D" H.T. Coy for transfer	7 h.m.
"			One other rank to 16.3 "D" H.T. Coy for transfer	7 h.m.
"	15.4.19	6 PM	Routine	7 h.m.
"	16.4.19	6 PM	Routine	7 h.m.
"	17.4.19	6 PM	Routine	7 h.m.
"	18.4.19	6 PM	Routine	7 h.m.
"	19.4.19	6 PM	Routine	7 h.m.
"	20.4.19	6 PM	Two other Ranks returned from detached Duty at H.Q.C.E.S.	7 h.m.
"	21.4.19	6 PM	Routine	7 h.m.
"	22.4.19	6 PM	Routine	7 h.m.
"	23.4.19	6 PM	Routine	7 h.m.
"	24.4.19	6 PM	Lt Col Robertson R.J.C. 850. R.A.M.C. demobilized & ordered to team F.A.S. taken ofdemob 24/4/19 3	7 h.m.

WAR DIARY
INTELLIGENCE SUMMARY

Army Form C.2118.

Place	Date	Hour	Summary of Events and Information	Remarks and references to Appendices
Saloniqe	25.4.19	6 PM	Three other ranks to Con. Camp for demob.	M.M.
	26.4.19	6 PM	Capt. E.mo R.A.M.C. struck off strength of unit for 29/3/19	M.M.
			A.D.M.S. 124 8/187 of 26.4.19	M.M.
	27.4.19	6 PM	Three other ranks to 63 B.M.T. Coy for duty	M.M.
			One other rank from 63 D.M.T. Coy for duty	M.M.
	28.4.19	6 PM	Three other ranks attached Battalion taken on strength of the unit. Two other ranks to Con. Camp to Struma Valley	M.M.
	29.4.19	6 PM	Routine.	M.M.
	30.4.19	6 PM	Routine.	M.M.

J.M. McCarthy Capt
R.A.M.C.